Days of the Trap

Days of the Trap

Freedom Is Just A Million Dollars Away

Johnny Mitchell

Published by Tablo

Copyright © Johnny Mitchell 2020.
Published in 2020 by Tablo Publishing.

All rights reserved.

This book or any portion thereof may not be reproduced or used in any manner whatsoever without the express written permission of the author except for the use of brief quotations in a book review.

Publisher and wholesale enquiries: orders@tablo.io

20 21 22 23 LSC 10 9 8 7 6 5 4 3 2 1

Table of Contents

A note from the author	1
Party Over	3
Two Hours Later...	7
Part I	9
The Sack	11
The Turf	19
The Connect	23
Invasion	29
Fish	37
Downey, CA	41
Fish: Part 2	47
Salvatore	53
Graduation	61
Part II	67
ATM	69
Filthy	77
Colombia	79
Maria	85
Promise	93
High speed	99
Interview	105
Part III	109
The Beast	111
Tres Letras	117

Bitch Slap	**123**
Goodbye	**129**
Apple Pie	**135**
Batter Up	**141**
Dirk	**153**
Shabazz	**161**
Jimmy	**167**
Sticking	**171**
Trouble	**177**
Disciples	**183**
Stand Up	**189**
Surgery	**195**
What's Beef?	**199**
Be	**203**
Keyholder	**207**
14 Grams	**213**
Epilogue	**219**
About the author	**227**

A note from the author

This is a story about my time spent in the Trap. "The Trap" refers to an underground economy as important to domestic output as any legitimate industry. It is fast disappearing as the century-old experiment of prohibition comes to end — but in its heyday, the Trap was one of the great wealth-generating activities in the modern history of capitalism.

This is one man's story set in the final days of the Trap.

The events which occur in this book were made possible by the things I have heard, seen, and — in many cases — participated in directly. It is a "novel" only in the sense that I have altered and embellished names, dates, and select instances for the sake of continuity and dramatic effect — and to protect the criminals who still haven't been caught.

It is written in a language meant to capture the spirit of the time, which is to say that it is colloquial, crass, unapologetic, and — by today's standard — offensive. I can live with that. The Trap is not a nice place, and neither is the world.

This book is dedicated to all the hustlers of earth, who would prefer to die standing on their own two feet.

-J.M, 2020

Party Over

This game is a motherfucker — listen up and I'll explain. Whoever said illegal was the easy way never had their wrists wrapped in steel, you can bet that. Bet they never moved work across the greater forty-eight, or made coke stretch during the drought, or got cleaned for their stash by some stick-up kids with a loaded .38 pointed at their head. It didn't feel easy living on the run, or hearing the gavel fall, or watching that man bleed to death on the yard. You see, the Trap is like a casino — you might hit a hot streak, but in the end it's the house that always wins. Better believe every dollar you earn in this game you pay back threefold.

It only looks easy now, as I soar high above the clouds.

2010 in the Pacific Northwest — a special moment in time no doubt. Blink and you'll miss it. While the rest of the country starves, we can't finish our plate. Walk down the street, and hundred-dollar bills can be plucked from the trees like Florida grapefruits. From the Mendocino mountains to the cul-de-sacs of northeast Portland, a miracle is taking place. It's as though God finally opened the rain clouds over a drought-scorched land, watching while his children slurp down every last drop. Like the mob of '20s prohibition or the Colombians of the early '70s, this is our moment in history — our chance to feast. Planes, trains, and automobiles are how the dope moves east and the money gets ferried back west. Pounds of high-grade from the Golden Triangle are fetching double-up wholesale prices in almost every state across this fair land, creating new millionaires overnight.

I am but a minnow in this feeding frenzy, but in this racket even a minnow can gobble down $20,000 a week, free and clear. Like Viet Cong guerillas on the Ho-Chi-Minh trail, so too does my merchandise follow a clandestine route from Humboldt to Portland to Jersey and on up the Eastern seaboard. Bricks don't even touch the scale anymore — they just come in through the front and leave out the back, moving with the speed and efficiency of the FedEx trucks that transport them. I don't touch them anymore, either. I let my soldiers take the risk while I count up the spoils.

Still can't believe my dumb luck. In less than a year's time, I'll be the owner of a million dead green guys and a hotel on the Colombian coast. Not that I didn't earn it — some folks enter the dope game with a silver spoon in their mouth. I got my start bagging out dime sacks in my parents' basement. Weed, coke, shrooms — whatever was winning. And up the ladder I clawed, surviving police raids and home invasions and my Dad flushing the product down the toilet, until finally, at twenty-four, I've got life by the back of the hair — skirt hiked up, thrusting with all my might. Criminal, or good American? Perhaps they're one and the same. I'm just carrying on tradition, from the Roosevelts to the Kennedys to the Genoveses — getting it while-the-fuck it's good.

Focus now, big fella — you haven't crossed the finish line just yet. There's still work to be done. Gotta stay alert — paranoia is a pusher's best friend. Trouble is, this money will lull you to sleep.

Seems like they always come for you when you're at your weakest. Like today, annoyed and hungover, my courier calls me while I'm still in bed to tell me he's sick, so now I'll have to make the collections myself. I've got two packages arriving from the East Coast in a few hours, and I still haven't packed for my flight to Cartagena this afternoon. Maria will throw a fit if I miss that flight — might even put out a contract on my head, quite literally. She'll think I'm cheating, and since I'd prefer my body not be riddled with bullets by some twelve-year-old kid wearing a soccer jersey on the back of a Ninja bike, I have to act fast. I lean over to the naked broad lying next to me and rustle her awake.

"Hey, time to go."

"What's the rush?" she groans.

"Colombians are coming to kill us," I say, ripping off the covers.

"Huh?"

She's a wreck alright. I hustle her out the door like a security guard on a shoplifter. This is Betty, the neighborhood squeezer — they say she could teach the wind how to blow. Poor gal. She's probably been shooed out of more apartments than a starving raccoon, but at least I let her see the sun come up this time.

"I can't do this anymore, Betty," I say. "I'm in love with someone."

"Yeah alright, whatever," she says, stuffing her bra inside of her purse. She turns around to look at me, smiling with last night's lipstick smeared on her two front teeth. "Should I call you sometime?"

"Definitely."

I kiss her on the cheek and slam the door shut.

Freedom at last. My head is throbbing as I hurriedly stuff clothing into a suitcase and shower off last night's improprieties. My place is all drug dealer — nothing but a king-size bed and a coffee table furnishing this thousand-square-foot penthouse overlooking the Willamette River on Portland's northeast side. I could live in anywhere in this city — have a loft in one of those douchey glass eyesores sprouting up all over the place like dandelions, but fuck that. I'm loyal to the soil. Northeast is my home — the only neighborhood in America where doctors and lawyers raise their kids next to crack houses. A true melting PIREX pot.

I grab my keys and light up last night's reefer. The medicine eases the fog in my brain as I watch the sun breaching the clouds, reflecting brilliantly off the downtown skyscrapers. Me and my kind are the last of a dying breed. Ten years from now, the Trap will be all but extinct. Weed storefronts will sit legally in every strip mall from Seattle to San Diego, and nationally, the underground wholesale market will be reduced to a sliver. The game is entering the bottom of the ninth, and I'm in scoring position — a million dollars just ninety feet away at home plate. This money will alter the course of history, setting the table so my heirs and generations beyond can eat.

All I need to do is not fuck it up.

Two Hours Later...

I fucked it up. Someone's been snitching alright, but a real boss never blames a snitch. He expects it, in fact, for man is weak and his loyalty flimsier than the paper on which he gives his sworn statement. Just hope it's not who I think it is — if that's the case, my whole empire is in jeopardy.

The pounding on the door is so loud it shakes the apartment, and in the distance, I hear the faint chop of the helicopter approaching. I take a deep breath and step off the edge of the balcony, aiming for the tall, unkept grass in the corner of the neighbor's lawn. I could surrender, but I'd rather make them earn it. That's what we pay taxes for — at least that's what I've been told by those who pay them.

Bullseye. I land squarely in the tall grass, my legs giving out from under me. I grab the duffel bag full of cash and begin sprinting through backyards, hurdling fences, and dodging clothes lines —ghetto track and field, as it were. I slow down, poking my head out from behind a garage. They've got the extraction team with the battering ram entering my apartment building now. I see my getaway car — the one I keep stationed on the block for occasions like these — parked just yards away. Feet fail me not — in less than a minute I'm throwing her into reverse.

"There he goes!" I hear one of the pigs shout.

Flooring her now, I'm speeding down the street in reverse like I'm reenacting Ronan. Stupid fucking cops forgot to block off the intersection. I look forward — the flashing red-and-blue is gaining fast. I plow through the stoplight at MLK and pull a three-pointer, chucking it into drive and punching the gas.

Flying down the Boulevard now, in my rearview I see one of the pigs spin out of control and crash into a parked car. I begin laughing like a madman, tears of joy and horror running down my cheeks. No wonder I don't see it coming. The suburban rams my bumper and now I'm the one spinning out of control — luckily that telephone pole is there to stop me. Now would be a good time to give up. The unmarked comes to a halt and the squad jumps out. They're drawn down, inching slowly toward me now, ready to make Swiss cheese.

"Lemme see your hands!" a copper yells.

Well done, boys. Well done.

And everything was so perfect just yesterday. Today, I'm cuffed in the back of this squad car as it glides gently through traffic on the way to the Multnomah County Jail. Going to miss my flight, Maria. It's Friday — won't be able to see the Judge and post bail until next week. I need to warn the connects in Jersey but I can't do it over the jail phone, and I've got at least $400,000 in exposed cash that has to be moved before the law finds it. My mind is spinning like a hamster wheel. Who's talking? Do they know about Colombia? I need to hurry up and solve this riddle before the whole house burns to the ground.

I lean my head back and close my eyes. Working on borrowed time, Johnny Boy. You'll make a nice display on the front page of the metro section tomorrow morning, no doubt. Then the neighborhood who raised you will finally get to witness the product of their environment. How did things ever get so far? Where did I go wrong? Hard to believe it all started with fourteen grams.

Part I

THE STREETS

2004-2007

The Sack

I'll never forget the day I fell in love with the Trap. How could I? It was also the day I got my first piece of cunt. Well, sort of.

It's the summer of '04, and me and CJ are at the dope man's door, asking for his blessing.

Only eighteen, but already I want out. Life — in all of its horror — is not something I want to participate in. To be true, horror to most people means genocide or starvation or a gaping hole in the ozone layer — for me, it means getting a job. Far as I can see it, the only reason for a sane man to take up a job is because he has to, and whenever a man is forced to do anything he does not want to do, then he is not free. Freedom is my highest ideal, and as I look around, I see the majority of man does not have it.

"Maybe it's just you, ya know? You're the laziest person I ever met," CJ said, as we passed the grape swisher back and forth that day on the bleachers by the baseball field, waiting for the world to end.

CJ is my better half. A moonfaced quadroon, his skin is mostly white but his full name is Charles Jerome —"on account of my Granddaddy, who was blacker than a motherfucker." We met sophomore year at Grant High School and instantly formed like Voltron. One of the greatest men I'll ever know, he's unlike me in almost every way, except for the devil he's got inside of him.

"You're missing the point," I said, choking on dope smoke like I'd been caught in a house fire. "There's two kinds of people in this world, CJ — cats who do what they wanna, and cats who do what they gotta."

He started laughing so hard he nearly fell off the bleachers. Some prick alright.

"That's a DMX quote, you idiot," he gasped between giggles, stoned tears flooding his face.

"You get my point, cocksucker," I said. "Money — THAT is the way to be free. We're out here getting high every day, meanwhile we're letting this money pass us by."

He nodded thoughtfully. "Everyone is getting high — always."

"We should be getting our taste," I said.

It was the irrefutable allure of street logic — when there's quick money on the line, you'd be a fool to pass it up.

He let the smoke trickle slowly out of his nostrils, scratching pensively at his peach fuzz.

"So, you really think you're a hustler?" he asked.

I grinned. "Don't doubt it."

I knock again on the iron bars fortifying the doorframe like a jail cell. Lucky to even be here, really. In the days of the Trap, low-level pushers didn't have access to middlemen the way they do now. It was a clandestine racket, and finding a distributor at wholesale wasn't as easy as an online search. The closer one came to the source, the more connected he had to be.

"What do you want?"

The Barry White-looking figure standing in the doorway grunts in a silky, baritone octave. A towering black man with a jerry curl permed past his shoulders – he's got on house slippers, a bathrobe, and cheetah-print underwear. In his right hand, adorned with gold rings, he dangles a nickel-plated .357 Magnum.

"We're friends with Antoine," CJ says. "He told us to come by, said you could help us out?"

He frowns suspiciously, his face scrunched up like a basset hound.

"Yeah, alright," he finally says. "Come on in."

He sets down his heat and unlocks the screen door.

"I'm Sweet Tea."

Sweet Tea is our friend Antoine's father. I've known Antoine since the '90s and Beaumont Middle School. He was one of those cats that became an O.G. by the time he was fourteen years old — motherfucker even let me hold his .22 pistol with the duct tape handle outside of gym class one day. Antoine's family are all original rockers, first-generation black immigrants who exported the crack trade from southern California to Portland in the mid-1980s. I still remember that sack of yellow stones he showed me one day after school.

"Eight hundred bucks, Johnny — all from these little pebbles," he smiled with pride. He still had braces on his teeth.

Now those pebbles have Antoine sitting in the Feds for a nickel, but before he got shipped out, he agreed to put in a word for us.

"Y'all had me scared, knocking on the door like you the goddamn po-lice," Sweet Tea mumbles as we enter the house. No matter how gingerly you do it, black people always think you knock like the cops.

Like all the old-timers, Sweet Tea has a diverse portfolio of hustles, not the least being high-grade indoor chronic. For years we'd also heard rumors that he was a pimp, about how he had a stable of hoes selling snatch for him even though he was still married to Antoine's mother. No one believed it though, not really — shit that cool never happens in Portland.

His pad is dimly lit and smells like a concoction of Caribbean oils and Nag Champa. The Isley Brothers echo softly from a record player spinning in the corner, and above the fireplace — surrounded by framed photos of his kids — he's got a Samurai sword on display. In the living room, right next to a big-screen TV, he's got a colorful fish tank bubbling with exotic fish. This is an old-school cat indeed.

"Have a seat," he beckons to a black leather couch. "What do you need?"

"A half," CJ says.

"Alright, I can do it for fifteen hundred."

"Fifteen hundred for a half-ounce?!" it comes shooting out of me.

"Oh man," Sweet Tea sighs, running his hand through his perm. The frustration of dealing with these two amateur gray boys is visibly agonizing.

"That's the ticket for half a POUND. If I'd known y'all was gonna interrupt my fuck session for a lousy half-ounce, I woulda never answered the door."

"That's our bad," CJ says, all cool-like. "This is the first sack we ever copped, and we wanted to test the market first."

"Alright, alright," Sweet Tea says. "You cats seem solid, and you know my son, so I'll hook you up today. But if you wanna keep fucking with me down the line, you're gonna need to get your order up, dig?"

"We can dig it," I say. "Don't expect anything less."

"Good," he nods, satisfied. "Aye yo Tracy! Monique!" he yells down the hall toward the bedroom. Then comes the sound of two purring kittens.

"Yes, Daddy?"

"Bring yo asses."

I hear the pattering of footsteps on the carpet, and then I see them — two Black Beauties, selected to win. Built like prized Arabian mares, these bitches are rap video fare. Wearing nothing but see-through silk panties, they let their perky D-cups bounce freely like Amazonian foragers.

So, the rumors are true! Sweet Tea is a pimp alright, and a damn good one at that — what with animals like these in his stable — and in Portland, of all places!

"Take care of our guests," Sweet Tea commands. "I'll be right back," before disappearing down the hall.

The girls have a seat on the couch between me and CJ. I've got a heat going something fierce, and I feel blood filling up my prick like a hypodermic needle.

"Whatever business y'all have sure must be important," one of them says, "cause Sweet Tea don't like to be interrupted while he's screwin'."

"Shit, neither do I," the other one says. "Y'all left us horny as hell."

"Girl!"

They giggle in that way whores do even though nothing funny's been said.

"So is he," CJ says, pointing at me. "He's never even been laid."

The bastard — he knows I'm self-conscious about that. I must be the last virgin left at Grant High School, and maybe in the entire state of Oregon. No way people will buy weed from a guy who's never had no pussy.

Of course, as soon as CJ said this the whores start clawing at me like vultures on a carcass. Now, I'm engulfed by brown flesh reeking wonderfully of cocoa butter while I suckle at their teats like a baby piglet.

Suddenly, one of the whores pulls out my swollen unit, mounting me like a gaucho on her trusty steed. I feel the lips of her cunt gripping my sword through her panties. She begins gyrating back and forth, groaning with pleasure. No way this'll last long. I fight as hard as I can, but it's useless — she's a powerful buck indeed. I unleash the goo, and it projectiles onto my chest and neck and a few drops splatter onto my cheek.

"That's it?" she says.

CJ falls to the floor, laughing so hard he has to clutch his sides.

"Congrats, Johnny!" he wails between hyena cackles.

"That'll be three hundred bucks," she says.

"Wait, what?"

"Oh, you thought this pussy was free?" she snaps, waiving an acrylic nail in my face.

"But, I didn't even put it in!" I protest.

"Run my motherfucking money, nigga!" she yells at the top her lungs.

Soon, all of us are shouting — CJ, the two naked whores, and me with my pants down, drenched in my own cum.

"Enough," the baritone-deep voice brings the room to a screeching silence. Standing there is Sweet Tea, holding the biggest bag of weed I've ever seen.

"They were trying to shake me down, Sweet Tea."

"Course they were. That's what I trained 'em to do." He snaps his fingers and the whores retire to the other room, cold mugging me as they leave.

"Get that bed warm for me," he says, cupping a handful of ass-cheek with his massive palm as they walk by.

"You'll have to excuse my bitches," he says, plopping down on a chair in front of CJ and I. "In the jungle, it's always the female lion that's more ferocious than the male one, you feel what I'm saying?"

He takes out a digital scale and reaches into the black garbage bag filled to the brim with smelly buds.

"Let that be lesson number one," he continues, filling up two sandwich bags and licking them shut. "All these distractions in life, but the only thing you need to keep your mind on is paper."

He pulls out a wad of hundred-dollar bills as thick as a baseball and tosses it onto the table.

"Where I'm from, we call it 'Go,'— G-O — and do you know why? Cause when you got it, it's a green light. You ain't got it? Shit, you're stuck at the red, Jack."

And so it went.

I'd been reluctant coming here today. After all, what chance did I really have of making a living in this fickle business? Sweet Tea just erased any doubt. He's got it all: money, a mean pad, and bad hoes. But most important is what he doesn't have – a job or a boss. If he can do it, then with any luck, I can too. Feels like my whole life has been a preview to this — the feature presentation. Hustler, drug dealer — who knows how far it'll take me.

Sweet Tea lights up a Marley spliff and passes it around.

"I'm giving you twenty-eight grams, a half an ounce each. You pay for one and I'll front you the other."

I pick up my half, clutching it in my palm like it's Hercules' globe. Fourteen grams to freedom.

"Gimme a call when you're ready to re-up," he says, walking us out the door. "And remember, show love to this game and it'll show it right back."

"Will do," I say, shaking his hand.

"And go wash that nut off your face."

The Turf

I'm shivering, the back of my palms itch and there's a glean in my eye. I'm dope sick alright, and only one way I know to get well.

Fall of '04 at the University of Oregon, and CJ and I are open for business. Ever the underachiever, I'd just managed to matriculate here by the skin of my nuts. Good thing I did — Eugene is a gold mine.

This isn't a town, or a campus, or an institution of higher learning. This is a territory, a market — a faceless, bottomless organism that gobbles up the product and spits out cash.

Like any business, the dope game is structured like a two-lane highway running up the side of a pyramid — shit travels downhill while the money moves up it. CJ and I started in the bottom of the shit.

The name of the game is clientele. Any wannabe can go and cop a pack — all that matters is if he can move it.

Distribution is a fascinating thing. How does every product of earth move from raw material to factory floor to supplier and finally, get swallowed up by an invisible consumer? And what if that product is outlawed? How does one scale a business that isn't allowed to exist? It all depends on the turf.

On the corners of west Baltimore and the *favelas* of Rio, crack and smack are sold in the open-air by crews of lookouts and runners, usually on consignment from older dealers who claim dominion over the corner and enforce it through economic power and violence. It is the most archaic, dangerous, and undemocratic way of selling drugs. In America, the open-air model is all but dead except for the most blighted areas, like the Tenderloin of San Francisco — places so densely populated and teeming with junkies that it makes sense for pushers to loiter at all hours of the day, as the traffic of fiends seeking out their fix is virtually nonstop.

The second model is the d-spot, or dope spot, invented in South Central during the crack explosion of the '80s after Reagan turned the heat up on street dealing. Instead of exposing oneself to the elements, better to barricade the business indoors and have the customers come inside to score. Every ghetto in America during the '80s and '90s had at least one crack house on every block. The d-spot style of slinging is still employed in government housing all over America. Like church or 7-Eleven, it is a reliable landmark of every impoverished neighborhood, open twenty-four hours a day for the dope fiends' convenience.

But by far the most civilized and ubiquitous means of distribution is curb-serving — or delivery. Technology and the advent of the cell phone opened a lane for middle-class dealers like CJ and I. No need to kill a man for his corner or stay up all night in a dirty trap house. Cell phones removed the need for brick-and-mortar institutions and democratized the buying and selling of narcotics. No more mafia-controlled monopolies, cheese lines, or bloody turf wars. The product *is* the advertisement — and may the best product win. Finally, a truly free market.

As it turns out, Eugene is the ideal place to get my dick wet. A major college campus is fertile turf for retail distribution. High density, trafficked with thousands of newly liberated young people — their pockets brimming with Mommy and Daddy and Uncle Sammy's money —looking to get lost in a nihilistic fog of weed, booze, and fat white pussy.

CJ's phone buzzes.

"It's my professor again. Fucking guy is my best customer," he says, pulling out two dub sacks from the shoebox below his bed. He grabs his skateboard and heads for the door.

"Hurry back so I can finish whooping your ass," I say, pausing Madden on the PlayStation.

Our dorm room serves as the headquarters of our fledgling little empire, still a pipe-dream no doubt. Pre-paid phones chirping steadily, day and night we traverse campus, trading dope for dollars. Sweet Tea's product is one helluva salesman, and it isn't long before we have to start making weekly visits back to Portland for the re-up.

From the jump, our strategy has been to undercut.

"I want all the clientele," I'd told CJ when we first set up shop. Like a sick junkie needs a soothing dose of heroin to ease his ills, so too do I need the reassuring feel of legal tender against my skin before I can rest well at night.

"You know how I can tell you're gonna go far in this business?" CJ said to me one day after watching me count out a stack for the third time in a row. "You love money more than drugs."

Indeed, a good drug dealer is far more addicted to the rush of quick cash than his customers are to his product. But it goes deeper than money alright — for the pusher, it's the game itself that holds an irresistible allure. With each sale, each re-up, each pack that gets swallowed up by the earth, for a brief moment in time it makes him all-powerful — God-like, even — for he has stood up to the omnipotent power of society and all the resources aimed at stopping him, and triumphed. He is an outlaw, a free bird. No surprise that the public at large is privately enamored of the outlaw. The average citizen — condemned to life in a cubicle — admires him, in fact, for it is he who has taken a good look at the world and the way things are and politely declined. "I think I'll do this my way," he says.

But it ain't all sweet — not by a long shot.

"There's a problem," CJ tells me one day after we'd finished off a pack.

Always a problem with him, but he's got a crooked eye by nature. He lives in reality, and I'm a dreamer.

"We're not making any money. We sell two ounces a week in twenty and forty bags, and we're lucky if we pocket two hundred bucks a piece."

He's quite right. It's the summer of '05, and my plan to undercut worked — almost too well.

You see, Oregon has always been flooded with the cheapest, highest quality marijuana in the country. Only a bad motherfucker can turn a profit here. Two classes of dealers exist in this era: premium pushers who sell top-shelf, indoor-grown pot at the highest prices, and commercial pushers who deal in mass-produced outdoor pot to be sold at lower prices.

Trouble with our business model is, we've combined the two. We're giving Sweet Tea $250 an ounce for drop dead, top-of-the-line indoor fire, but then turning around and retailing it at commercial prices. Now, our transaction rate to profit margin is laughably lopsided. In my lust to acquire clientele, I'd reduced our take to beer and sneaker money.

"It goes against the laws of economics, and logic," CJ says. "We've got champagne and we're giving it away like malt liquor."

"I know, but now we've got the customers," I say. "What we need to do now is level up. No more hand-to-hand sales. We become the dealers' dealer and start wholesaling our packs."

"We're gonna need a bigger supply and a lower price — a lot lower. And we ain't gonna get that from Sweet Tea."

"Nope," I say, shaking my head. We've outgrown the old pimp. Time to get to the source. "We need to find a grower."

The Connect

"Lift your shirts up for me please," he says, the twang in his voice like an old guitar string.

They stare at us, unflinching — two hillbillies in overalls with shotguns resting over their shoulders — and suddenly, I'm reminded of the movie *Deliverance*. I glance at CJ. Surely, he looks more like a pig than me, right?

We're hours away from anything, deep in the Klamath National Forest at the southernmost tip of the state. Down the hill and across a small valley, we see California. Beneath our feet is God's country, the center of the Universe, the nucleus around which all life revolves. This is the northern tip of the Golden Triangle, the region where nine out of every ten pounds of domestic marijuana distributed throughout the nation originates.

We shrug, then lift up our shirts. No police wires — just pale, hairy beer bellies. The polite man nods and spits a gooey load of chew into the dirt.

"Whaddaya say, Ralph? These boys good?" he asks the officer leaning against his cruiser.

He nods.

"Followed them up from the five. They're alone."

These bumpkins mean business alright. We'd been directed to meet at a bar on the outskirts of Ashland, a small border town three hours south of Eugene off of Interstate 5. Almost shit my pants when a local pig in uniform was there to meet us.

"You must be Johnny and CJ," he said, sidling up next to us at the bar. "Shot of whiskey," he muttered to the barkeep. He tossed it down the hatch, wiped his mouth, then turned to us.

"Follow me."

Making sure we didn't have a tail, he proceeded to escort us out of town and deep into the backcountry, almost two hours up winding, unpaved roads that nearly ruined my 1990 Acura Legend.

Now, finally — we stood at the gates of Rome.

The polite man nods, smiling at us through tobacco-stained teeth.

"Very well, then. My name's Kenny, and this here's my brother Walt," he beckons to the squat, pugnacious man standing next to him.

Walt nods and tips his John Deere hat, a chew the size of a golf ball jutting from his lower lip. There's something frightening about him but I can't quite make out what it is. Then I see it — he's got a glass eye, *sans* pupil, sticking out of his head like a cue ball.

"This way, fellas," he says.

After 1980, imported Colombian marijuana — which until then had supplied most of the American market — was put out to pasture by the Mexican cartels, who could grow it better and move it faster. Over the next thirty years, Mexican pot would itself die a slow death, this time at the hands of domestic growers like Kenny and Walt from Southern Oregon and Northern California. Not that the Mexicans gave up, they simply migrated north, setting up shop in the new Golden Triangle.

Now, an ideal climate and thousands of acres of public and private land was being exploited by growers of all stripes, with large criminal syndicates like the Sinaloa Cartel churning out thousands of pounds a year, down to the family-owned outfits producing a few hundred. This is the source, the supply — as high up the chain as a dealer could go. In the days of the Trap, it was every pusher's dream to meet a grower, for just one of these connections could elevate him from hand-to-hand sales to weight-supplier overnight. It was like being admitted to an exclusive club, one with high membership dues — five thousand dollars to be exact — financed by CJ's student loan check. That was the cost of the introduction to Kenny and Walt, brokered by a family friend of Kenny's whom I'd met at a party in Eugene. It was winter of '06, a year and a half after CJ and I began the search for a new supplier. We were living in a small apartment off campus and still nickel-and-diming Sweet Tea's overpriced product.

"We're gonna make this back tenfold," I promised CJ. "This is the connect. No more small-timing. We're about to become the man."

The middleman, that is — the modern mercantilist tasked with moving goods from supplier to consumer. Only a handful of dealers in Eugene have connections with the growers in Southern Oregon. Every week, they make the drive south on I-5 and return north the same day with their trunks loaded. This return trip north is where the arbitrage happens, where prison time is risked, and where the real money is made. It's time to start making real money.

We follow Kenny through a passage of trees and down a steep trail toward an old barn sitting at the base of the property. We pass a burnt-out Volkswagen bug parked on the side of the trail, so old it seems like a natural feature of the landscape.

"Take no offense at the security measures," Kenny says. "Standard procedure."

Walt flanks us from the rear, his shotgun at the ready, as though CJ and I are court martialed soldiers being paraded to the gallows.

"We've had some issues lately," Kenny says. "Trusted friends who broke the code, chose to work for the other side."

We hear a helicopter flying low in the distance.

"Feds," he mutters, not bothering to look up.

"Plus, the Spics... ever since they come north from Sinaloa to set up grows, this area's been hot. A few of those bastards even tried robbing us, but — I s'pose that's the beauty of owning all this land," he pauses, gazing out over the expanse of the countryside. "Easy to make a fellow disappear."

He spits tobacco juice into the dirt and glances over at Walt, who grins for the first time.

I should've been frightened, but instead I just got more excited, like Karen in "Goodfellas" after seeing Henry Hill pistol whip her neighbor — a real whore for the rush. Besides, a man serious enough to kill is a man serious enough to do business with, and we're in no position to take the moral high ground — not after two years of scaping by selling twenty-dollar pops.

We reach the barn, which looks ready to fall over any minute. Kenny flips a switch and the lights come on, revealing the reason for our visit. Hanging end to end from the ceiling are rows of fully mature, fifteen-foot-high weed plants with buds the size of cow dung sagging off of them.

"Harvest came early this year," Kenny says, touching one of the plants lovingly. "Reckon we'll get close to five hundred pounds once it's all finished drying."

"We'll take it," I say, only half kidding.

"Works for me," he smiles. "I can sell these in Ashland for three grand all day, but for friends of Chris, I can go as low as, say, twenty-eight?"

"What are you, nuts?" CJ blurts out. "We could pay three thousand in Eugene and save ourselves the trip."

The sack on this guy! He fancies himself a regular Tony Montana, negotiating with Sosa at his Bolivian hacienda.

"You want the merchandise to move fast, right?" CJ continues. "It's better for everyone that way. But things aren't how they used to be, ya know? Nowadays, everyone and their mother is sitting on weight. Plus, we're the ones who gotta drive that shit up the interstate — that puts us at risk."

Kenny smirks, impressed by the audacity. CJ, that motherfucker — he's always found a way to get what he wants. He's likeable and well-respected, and he's got an intangible air of authority that draws people to him — qualities I don't possess. Indeed, I can't do this without him.

Kenny turns to look at his brother Walt, whose glass eye is twitching excitedly. He nods.

"Well," Kenny says, looking back at us. "I reckon we can work something out."

We wave goodbye now as I pull the Acura out of the driveway and proceed down the mountainside with the cop car trailing behind us.

At $2,300 a pound for top-quality commercial product, we can't lose. We'll become the dealers' dealers' dealer. It was that simple — just one little favor on behalf of the Universe, and now things will never be the same.

"Just one problem," I say to CJ as we lumber down the bumpy dirt road. "Where are we gonna get an extra thirteen grand?"

"Not sure yet. I didn't think that far ahead."

Kenny and Walt had agreed to a sale price of $2,300 per pound, but on the condition that we buy ten pounds or more at a time. After all our scrimping and saving, CJ and I had only $10,000 in the operating account, leaving us well short of the $23,000 needed for the first purchase. They'd told us to return in three weeks, after the weed had been dried and trimmed and ready to move.

There's no time to waste. Growers like Kenny and Walt have wholesalers driving in from all over the country to pick up merchandise. I'd even heard of dealers from out-of-state descending onto the Triangle during harvest season and buying up a grower's entire yield in one trip.

In the days of the Trap, when the supply of marijuana on the market was still finite — once a grower sold out of his stock — it meant just that, *no mas* . Then, his wholesalers would be left scrambling to find other growers. After all, a dope dealer ain't much good to nobody without any dope to sell.

"I've got an idea," I say to CJ, though I don't speak it aloud. It's the only thing that comes to mind for a pusher in need of a quick cash injection. The old-fashioned way. The ski mask way.

Invasion

This game is a motherfucker, and boy I ain't never lied. You worship the ground it walks on all these years, and then finally it shows you some love back. Now you're out here getting money — you probably even think shit is sweet, don't you? That's when the tax man appears, demanding his cut. He doesn't send you a bill, either. Your money or your life, punk — one way or another, you're gonna run that shit. Speaking of someone who owes too much to the game, this loaded .38 cocked inches from my face has me thinking I might have some unpaid debt.

His adrenaline is kicking, breath coming heavy, and through the eye sockets in his ski mask, I see his pupils darting frantically left to right. An old fashioned Jooks is underway — a jack, a lick, a kick-door — a motherfucking home invasion. I'd give anything to be on the other side of that gun, if only for the thrill. You have to admire the set of nuts on these two — broad daylight on one of the busiest streets in Eugene. Caught us with our pants down alright, but that's how the game goes — always when you're at your weakest.

We'd been in the living room at the time, four of us gathered around the TV playing a spirited game of Mario Kart for Nintendo 64 — our favorite pastime aside from the drinking and the whoring.

"Bet me fifty on this one, pussy," CJ slaps down half-a-C on the coffee table in front of me.

"Make it a hundred," I say, tossing out another fifty. "I get to be Toad."

"Fuck that, he's the best character. I'll be Donkey Kong and you be Bowser."

The gale banter of two assholes who have no clue their fortune is about to pivot on a dime.

Shit is good right now — too good, in fact. It's spring of '07 and Kenny and Walt's bricks are moving like clockwork. We've leveled up alright — you want a bag of weed to smoke, you better call someone else. Our clientele has thinned to a handful of lieutenants who take the work from us in quarters, halves, and whole pounds, then disperse them onto the invisible market. It took a few months after our initial meeting in Southern Oregon to get straightened out, but once we were, it was full steam ahead.

Each week we rotate, CJ or myself, making the drive south under the protective blanket of darkness with a duffel bag full of cash, then return north hours later with ten fluffy pounds of immaculate merchandise stuffed inside of it. Once again, the plan is to undercut — I want all the pushers on my team. Soon, we're clearing over $2,000 in profit a week, more than we could make in three months selling crumbs for Sweet Tea.

"We're fucking rich," CJ mused one day after throwing a fresh thousand stack into the fireproof safe.

He wasn't wrong. Barely twenty-one years old, and we were each making a teacher's salary off of our humble little trade. The way things are going I won't even need to get a summer job. This is all I've ever wanted — freedom. I didn't waste it.

I stopped going to class almost entirely — after all, what could my professors tell me if I'm already doing better than them? Besides, I'm probably hungover from last night when I drank until the lights went black. No more virgin Johnny, either — I'm stuffing my nub into every sloppy cow who will have me. Life is a feast and every day is like Thanksgiving.

No wonder I didn't see it coming.

There's a loud knock on the front door, and then the creaking sound of it swinging wide open. Nothing unusual about this — we often leave the door unlocked during the day for the constant stream of friends and roommates coming and going.

"Anybody home?" a man's voice yells out.

"Who is it?" CJ calls back, but by then they're already standing in the living room — two black-clad figures wearing ski masks and Timberland boots. The taller one's got a .45 and the shorter one a snub nose .38, the midnight special. It's an invasion alright — don't get no realer than this.

"Uhhh, can I help you?" CJ says, like he's waiting tables.

"Where the fuck is it?!" the tall one screams.

"Where's what?"

He's barely got the question out before a snuff across the chin sends him sprawling to the floor.

"The fucking work!" the man yells as he unloads his Timberland into CJ's ribs.

"Check the basement," the shorter one says.

Without hesitating, the tall one heads for the basement entrance next to the kitchen. Ah, so they've been in the house before? Makes sense — to have the drop on someone like these two have on us requires inside information. Could be anyone — a competitor, a disgruntled customer, or a pair of wolves who smelled dinner. Or maybe, just maybe, this is payback.

"Everybody on the fucking floor!" the short one commands.

Kissing dirty carpet now, I think back to the Oriental kid. Karma is playing out before my eyes.

After returning from our meeting with Kenny and Walt in Southern Oregon, we'd gone on the prowl for a victim. We needed investment capital fast — $13,000 — before they sold off their supply to another dealer. Since neither of us had a relative who would loan us the cash, that left only one other option: the Jooks.

The Jooks was common in the days of the Trap, accepted as a legitimate reality of the game like cops and droughts and price fluctuations. Even in an airy college town like Eugene, pushers were getting ripped-off on a weekly basis. For the small timers and the hobbyists, getting robbed usually forced them into retirement, either financially or because they lacked the heart for retaliation. But for career knuckleheads like CJ and I — men with stunted frontal lobes predisposing us to criminal behavior — the hunted simply became the hunters.

The most common form of this predation was the sneak attack, or the kick-door — stalk your prey and wait for him to leave the house, then bust in and snatch his work. The Jooks, on the other hand, was for adults only. The law of the jungle must be obeyed when committing armed robbery, namely, that you only Jooks someone less dangerous than yourself. Pull a Jooks on someone willing to die for their product, and you've got a dilemma alright — a choice to make. Are you bluffing, or are you prepared to kill? Herein separates a gangster from everyone else.

"That's him," I said, pointing to the short yellow man walking up to his building.

We were staked out across the street in Murph's Oldsmobile, CJ behind the wheel and me and Murph in the backseat. Murph was a hitter we knew from the old neighborhood, a real grimy-type cat who didn't bat an eye when I told him about the job. We decided to leave CJ in the car as a lookout — he might not know it himself, but he's too clean for the dirt about to take place.

Murph let a Newport dangle from his mouth as he wiped down the barrel of his .22 Beretta.

"You say he's got pounds in there?"

I nodded, "Indoor, too — straight fire. You could flip em' for four grand a piece, easy."

"And you sure he ain't gotta crew?"

"Nope. Lives alone."

"Two billion Chinese in this world and he's the one with no friends?"

"I think he's Japanese. Or Filipino, maybe."

"Those are polar opposite Asians."

"Why's it matter what Asian he is?" CJ asked.

"Because, you ignorant mufucka," Murph snapped, "the Japs have a docile culture. They're raised to be obedient — comes from Confucianism. If he's Japanese, he'll give it up quietly. But the Filipinos are jungle Asians. They're like us niggas — they roll deep and they're scrappy. If he's Filipino, he might put up a fight."

"How do you know so much about Asian culture?"

"Community college. I took a class on Eastern philosophy last semester — fascinating shit."

"Trust me, Murph," I said. "I've been casing the spot for two weeks. The kid's a loner — he doesn't even keep his bricks in a safe."

I should know, I used to do business with him. He would sell me work if I needed something in a pinch and Sweet Tea was unavailable. He was a nerd alright, but it's always the unassuming one's — not the tough guys — who make for great drug dealers. Pity I have to put him under now, but all is fair in love and war.

Murph flicked his Newport out the window, then reached over the seat and handed his gun to CJ.

"Hold this. I'm not gonna need it."

Dressed in all black, we slipped on our leather burner gloves and readied our ski masks. I looked up at the light flickering on from his second story window.

"He's Japanese," I said. "He's gotta be."

Five minutes later, I was on the floor of this kid's apartment — fighting for my life. Either he wasn't Japanese, or I'd greatly underestimated the resolve of the Japanese people.

Ski masks down, we'd shoved our way inside of the apartment he hadn't bothered to lock. We found the kid sitting on his couch smoking a joint next to another Asian man, only this one was built like a nose tackle. They sat there stunned for a split second, giving Murph time to take out his billy club — the kind the police use during riots. As the large one charged at us, Murph swung the club, connecting cleanly against the side of the man's head. He dropped to the floor with no more than a grunt.

I looked over at the little one, who was reaching for something underneath the couch. I didn't wait to see the gun, I just rushed — tackling him onto the floor. I tried to put him in a headlock, but he was slippery alright. He wiggled out of it and grabbed my arm, twisting it behind my back until it felt like it was about to snap. I managed to elbow him in the ribs with my free arm, breaking his hold, then I wrestled him to the ground. I squeezed his neck in the crook of my elbow as hard as I could, until I felt his body go limp. I eased up, but then he surprised me with a shot to the kidney that left me writhing in pain. He got up and grabbed me around the neck with both hands. Through the eye sockets of my ski mask I could see the boiling fury in his face. He was trying to choke me and remove my mask at the same time, but then the loud cock of a gun stopped him in his tracks. Murph had the barrel of the kid's own jammy pressed against the back of his head.

"Get up, nigga," he said. "Slowly."

He did as he was told. I stumbled to my feet, panting horribly. I looked over at the big man lying on the ground — Murph had hogtied him with duct tape. With the gun still trained on him, I quickly did the same to the small one. Once we had them both on the floor incapacitated, we went searching for the goods.

Jackpot. In the kitchen below the sink, we uncovered the buried treasure — eight pounds of the highest-end Kush on the market, plus one pound of magic mushrooms. After selling it off and splitting the take with Murph, we'd have more than enough to make our first purchase with Kenny and Walt. It was a revolution alright — one that would launch CJ and I into a higher tax bracket.

We loaded the bricks into two separate duffel bags along with the men's cell phones, and Murph stashed the small one's piece inside of his waistband. I opened my knife and reached down, putting little cuts into the duct tape that bound their ankles. In an hour or two, they'd be able to wiggle their way free. Then we left as quickly as we had come, disappearing into the night.

Strange, isn't it? How easily a man is able to forget his sins, and his audacity of indignation at the very same sins when they return to exact vengeance upon him. Just six months after we'd put the yellow kid out of business, now here we are, getting taken to the cleaners.

I look closely at the short one in the ski mask swinging his gun wildly left to right. They'd caught us slipping, whoever they are. Normally we'd never keep the work in the house like this — it had only been temporary while we scouted out a new stash spot. Must be six pounds in the safe right now, and another $10,000 or so in cash, a nice little haul indeed.

"Don't look at me!" he yells and marches over to where I'm seated on the ground, shoving the .38 special so close to my face I could kiss the barrel.

The tall one comes lumbering up the stairs and into the living room.

"Found the safe!" he yells breathlessly to his accomplice. "I need the code."

The short one turns to me. "Gimme the fucking code!"

I look over at CJ and my roommates, who look back at me. They aren't scared, just waiting on me to decide. There's four of us and two of them. They've got guns but we've got solidarity, like scrappy Frenchman resisting Nazi occupation.

Slowly, and with my hands in the air, I stand up.

"Sit your ass down!" the short one screams, but panic has audibly overtaken his bravado.

"Don't anyone fucking move!" the tall one yells. He walks over to me and points the cannon squarely at my temple. "GIVE. ME. THE. CODE."

Is he prepared to do it? And am I prepared to find out? That's what this gangster shit boils down to. Since he's the invader, the burden of proof is on him to show us the gangsterism he purports to have. Trouble is, he just might. And since I'm in love with this hustling shit, the important thing is that I live to hustle another day. Besides, my roommates are civilians, and I'll have some explaining to do if one of them gets clipped behind a plant that old ladies smoke for their cataracts.

I stare down death through the barrel of that long-nose .45, looking as wide as a train tunnel. I nod my head slowly and let a smile curl onto my lips.

"Well done, boys. Well done."

Fish

From these green leaves, so bland and bitter as to be nearly insufferable, there shall appear a magic dust that will one day rule the world and bring even the Devil himself to his knees. No Incan prophet could have foretold the impact of the Fish.

Patient but not pushy, like the serpent gently teasing Eve with the apple, so too does the hook of the Fish reel you in slowly — so much so that most don't even realize they're hooked.

Odd how such a tepid buzz can cause ordinary people to do the strangest things — make a hyper person mellow and a mellow person hyper, turn complete strangers into old friends, even incline a whole generation to mix it with baking soda and deep throat it through a glass pipe.

And for what? No one can really tell you — that's the magic of it. I suppose that's why the Colombians who introduced Fishscale to the world in the early '70s were referred to as *Mágicos,* or Magicians, for with a wave of their wand they turned the chalky white rock — barely stronger than a cup of dark roast —into a business bigger than U.S. Steel.

I'm proud to be on the front lines of the Fish trade, the port of entry for the dollars arriving off the street that will eventually ascend the invisible ladder until they're resting safely in a Panamanian bank account. Spokes like me are what keep the wheel turning, same as any industry. The only person more important than me is this bitch hunched over the table with the jaw that won't stop moving.

"Toxic masculinity and gender inequality are the inevitable bi-products of neoliberalism," she says, before leaning over and making the white line disappear through a rolled-up Washington's face.

Fourth time tonight I've been through here, a party of yammering white women drinking craft beer and discussing intersectional feminist politics while they suck up the Fish like a Hoover vacuum.

Thursday through Sunday I'm on call 'til the wee hours, burner phone chirping non-stop like a bird's nest. Frat houses, study sessions, strip clubs, hospitals — I even have the Ducks' star linebacker and future NFL draft pick coming through to cop. These anonymous but invaluable men and women are the true heroes in the war on drugs — fighting bravely against the politicians and federal agents who wish to curb North America's appetite for the snort. Every dollar they spend with me helps fight poverty in rural Peru, bolster employment in the barrios of Medellin and Barranquilla, spurn investment and infrastructure on the frontiers of northern Mexico, and line the pockets of countless border patrol agents, cops, lawyers, bankers, judges, and merchants spanning the seven continents.

"Do you have any more?" the woman asks playfully, cozying up next to me on the couch as I drink a beer.

"Sure, it's seventy for the gram or one-twenty for two," I say, digging into my pocket.

At $70 a gram, I thought I was getting away with murder, until I learned that sniff of similar quality sells for $100 a shot in major cities like New York and Los Angeles.

"All I have left is twenty dollars," she says. "Is it okay if I pay you later?"

She's gonna make me laugh alright. I shake my head, shoving the stones back into my pocket.

"Nope."

Sorry, sweetie, but in the snow biz, it's C.O.D.

"Pleaaase!" she giggles and bats her eyelashes, her bare thigh rubbing up against my leg.

She's got me pegged as someone who capitulates to the cat, but she doesn't know me at all. The only ingredient truly necessary for success in the cocaine business is a passionate, unabashed love for money — and I love it alright, more than cocaine and cunt combined.

"You better go find an ATM," I say, checking my burner phone. I got moves to make.

"Hit me when you're right," I say, getting up from the couch.

A shaggy haired kid in a polo shirt enters the living room. His eyes are pools of ink, like a Great White when it attacks at the surface.

"This is great shit dude!" he exclaims, rubbing his gums fiendishly. "Where'd you get it?"

Downey, CA

The machete fell clean, slicing open the brick like a Saudi sword on the head of an infidel. Hector grabbed the rectangle with both hands and opened it neatly in half, holding out the two white chunks like an ice cream sandwich.

Distribution is a fascinating thing, isn't it? How a product can zig-zag around the world in search of its customers, and the dizzying array of human connections and cooperation necessary for its arrival.

As I stared at this ice cream sandwich, wrapped snuggly in cellophane with the unmistakable scorpion of the Sinaloa cartel stamped on the front, I thought about how many miles it had to travel to be here — by land, air, and sea — hidden in the hull of a ship, stored in boxes behind the pilot's seat of a single-engine Cessna, and buried deep inside the panels of an eighteen-wheeler, all while being pursued by the greatest law enforcement apparatus the world has ever known. Now, it was up to me to ensure safe transport to its final destination — the hungry noses of a thousand invisible consumers — thus completing the arduous lifecycle of the Fish.

"*Ju* see…" he said, pointing to the rigid grooves of the kilo, a yellowish hue tinting the snow-white flakes. "*Puro* Fishscale."

After a breathless pause, Brendan looked at me giddily, like a dog about to get a treat.

"Alright, Papi!" he yelled, giving Hector a high five. From the next room, a baby started whimpering.

"*Cállate, jüey,*" Hector held a finger to his lips, but Brendan could care less.

"You see?" Brendan said, punching me playfully in the arm. "Didn't I tell you this guy was legit!?"

"Yeah man. Don't wake up the baby."

"*Ju* wan' it straight up? Or *ju* wan' that I cut it?" Hector asked. "For *puro*, is twelve hundred an ounce, *pero* if you wan' me to cut it down, is eight hundred."

We ran some quick numbers and settled on the product with a little cut. Even at eighty percent pure, nothing else in Eugene would come close. Selling $70 grams, we could double up on each ounce. We'd make more on this one run than I could make in two months selling weed.

After getting stuck by the masked men in our living room, CJ and I went into hiding. We'd been taken for over half our net worth and had therefore been demoted back to small-time shitheads. We asked Kenny and Walt for some consignment, but by that time they'd already sold out of their harvest. With summer fast approaching and the overall supply in Southern Oregon dwindling, the wholesale price of the pound was going up and up.

CJ decided it was a good time to take a vacation, fleeing to Spain to study for a semester. I took quarter in a tiny two-bedroom house on the outskirts of campus, directly next door to our mutual friend Brendan Spader. With cash reserves low, I needed to restructure the business or risk going broke by the time CJ returned from Spain.

Brendan and I settled into the living room couch and let the chef get to work. It was midnight, and we'd just completed the fifteen-hour trek south from Eugene to Los Angeles. I assumed he was full of shit, Brendan and his whole rap about an *ese* he knew who was getting kilos delivered from the border straight to his door. But when we arrived at the house in East LA and found it guarded by two massive *cholos* with Uzis tucked into their Dickies, I knew then we were on to something.

A woman, presumably Hector's *mujer*, appeared from the back room carrying the sniffling baby.

"*Buenas ,*" she greeted, then plopped the baby down in its crib next to the couch. "*¿ La puedas guardar ?*"

"*Sí ,*" I answered.

A weird fucking day this was shaping up to be.

Moments later, the woman returned from the kitchen carrying two cold *Pacíficos* . In the other hand, she held a large butcher knife with four evenly sliced helpings of Fish resting on the blade. We each took turns treating our nostrils, sniffing and gulping and gasping. It was pure Fish alright, fresh from the sea — untouched since its conception in a Colombian jungle.

She left a baggie of powder for us to enjoy, then assumed her position as Hector's sous-chef in the kitchen. They had the recipe down like it was mother's apple pie: eighteen ounces of pure cocaine were weighed out on a digital scale, then four were subtracted. The fourteen ounces of pure were scrambled with eight ounces of various cutting agents — of what I'm not exactly sure — this is what makes the recipe a secret. Generally, the Fish is known to be diluted with caffeine pills and other GNC products like creatine and boric acid. During the drought season when inventory is scarce, this cut is increased, making the Fish stretch like Silly Putty. But not today. Hector and his lovely assistant were causing a snowstorm in the middle of June.

The Fish had me gone alright. My ticker was thumping fiercely, and my head felt like it was floating away on a hot-air balloon. I looked over at Brendan, his beak was feasting on the white earthworms like a seagull on the beach at low tide. He looked back at me, beaming, his glassy green eyes dancing wildly with excitement.

"We're gonna take over the town with this shit, Johnny Boy," he said, rubbing the powdered sugar into his gums. "Just watch — next time we come down here, we're gonna cop a whole fucking kilo!"

I like Brendan, known him since freshman year when we were both wannabes running around campus selling reefer sacks. He's a San Diego surfer bro with a nasty hustle — plus, he's connected — better suppliers and bigger clientele than me or CJ. Trouble with Brendan is, he's a cowboy, a livewire — moving at Lamborghini speed with the headlights off. Also, he ain't family, and in the Trap, the most dangerous thing a man can do is go into business with someone who ain't family.

Still, as I stood on my stoop that day, listening while he pitched me his new hustle, I realized it was the last hope me and CJ had for saving our floundering enterprise.

"Don't be a putz, Johnny!" he chuckled, passing me the trippy-stick. A garrulous fuck, he could talk a cat down from a fish wagon. "You were moving all that weed, and for what? A couple grand a month? Chicken feed compared to what I'm talking about."

"That chicken feed was keeping us full," I said, coughing on the stick. "The Fish is a different animal. It's too risky."

"Too risky? What do you call getting robbed at gunpoint? With coke, you can move a quarter of the quantity for double the profit. We'll never even have to wholesale, just move it rock for rock."

He was right, retailing Fish was more lucrative than wholesaling weed, and if we sold only to users, we'd reduce the risk of another invasion by bandits or the cops.

"Why'd you come to me?" I asked. "There's plenty of guys out there with money who'd go half with you."

"It's not just about the money, it's about balls. This business takes big fucking balls. Most people in this town either don't have 'em or won't use 'em. But me and you do, and that's why we're gonna win."

He was slick alright, getting me tree-top high while he gassed my ego like a Chevron attendant. I hit the stick one more time, staring off into the distance.

"Let me talk to CJ," I said, though I already knew his answer.

"Yeah, you talk to CJ, then call me tomorrow. We go to LA next week to meet the connect."

He grinned at me, the way a car salesman does when he knows he's roped a sucker.

"There's easy money to be made, Johnny. You'd be stupid to pass it up."

And there it was: hook, line, and sinker — the number one immutable commandment of the Trap.

The baby whimpered again. I adjusted its pacifier and tickled its little foot with my finger. It was a girl I assumed, from the earrings and the pink jumper. She studied me curiously between rich, dark-brown eyes, like an alien who appeared from thin air taking in the strange creatures of her new planet. I leaned down and kissed her on the forehead. Baby smell is so wonderful, so pure — like stepping into a brand-new car for the first time. Tragic how quickly this new smell dissipates as the stench of life seeps its way under the skin.

Brendan shoved more candy under my nose — sniff, sniff. My jaw was glued-shut and paranoia on code red. I'll take another one, if you don't mind. The greatest trick the Devil ever pulled was making you want more and more without knowing why.

Baby girl kept on staring at me, making my palms sweat. What did she have on me? Hopefully she can keep a secret.

It was almost three in the morning by the time the cake was done baking. After running it through a strainer, Chef Hector stuck the white square into the microwave. Ten minutes to let it air out, and then he weighed the finished product — just over twenty-two ounces. Wrapping it tightly in plastic, Hector handed the block to Brendan, who passed him a stack of bills. A quick check, $14,500 — all accounted for.

As we turned to leave, I looked back one last time at the baby girl. She was still staring at me, unblinking — a witness to the evil of man before she was even able to speak.

We shook hands with Hector.

"See you next month," I said.

A week later, we were back in his living room.

Fish: Part 2

This game is a motherfucker, are you beginning to see it now? It's like dating a whore who's out of your league — the minute you think she loves you, the minute she has you convinced she's changed her ways, is the minute she sneaks off to bed with a finer stag.

It's noon when I open my eyes. Don't remember passing out, just a stack of crumpled twenties and fifties on my nightstand to remind me of the dirt that's been done. Sunday morning, and licks have been knocking steady since Thursday night. I peer through the blinds at the neighbor's backyard. Brendan is sitting Indian-style on the lawn, meditating with a joint hanging from his lips. He's got red war paint smeared under his eyes and seems to be chanting some sort of indigenous tune.

"This nigga's crazy," I mutter aloud.

Must still be in the throes of his acid trip. He loves that shit, but it hasn't stopped him from turning his house into a drive-through window for cocaine.

Day and night, the bubbleheads stay knocking on his door — as he predicted they would. Hector's dope was an atomic bomb. It's the end of the summer, and we've already been back to see him four times. Packs are moving so fast we've had to start increasing the cut to avoid making that excruciating drive every week. I've doubled the money we lost to the invasion and then some, and best of all, CJ is getting home next month. Harvest season is around the corner, and I can hardly wait to return to the Golden Triangle to see what Kenny and Walt have yielded for us.

I lounge on the stoop in my underwear, dropping cigarette butts into an empty bottle of Old English 800. It was only supposed to be a temporary gig, but I'm eating way too tough to quit now. The power of the Fish is irresistible alright, stringing me along helplessly on its hook. Besides, this is a smart business move — diversification is crucial, like Warren Buffet says. Too much volatility in this game to be relying on a singular product. I'll let CJ handle the weed while I manage the blow, this way we'll be well-positioned the next time disaster strikes.

"Johnny Boy!" Brendan stumbles onto my stoop bare chested, his man tits flopping about like loose pancakes. "What's up baby boy?"

"All's well. I'm almost sold out again."

"Yeah, me too. They can't get it fast enough."

He re-lights his spliff and passes it to me.

"Do you ever think what we're doing is wrong? I mean morally, that is."

"What else could you mean?"

"I was watching this thing on the Discovery Channel last night about how they make cocaine in the jungle. Turns out even the purest shit is still really bad for you."

"Buddy, if you insist on talking like this, I'm afraid I'm gonna have to ask you to leave."

"Look, I know there's levels of right and wrong, and certainly if they didn't get it from us, they'd find it somewhere else, but does that make it right?"

"Of course it's wrong, fucko!" I snap.

I've heard just about enough of this moral vacillation. I'm riding high on the thrill of life and this prick wants me to confront my disreputable behavior — and on a Sunday no less.

"Listen, pal. Me and you, we're not men of upstanding moral character. That's just the way it is, and thank God for it. If everyone chose to do the moral thing, how would people get their drugs?"

"Wow, that was incredible," he replies, lifting up his shades and staring at me through acid-washed eyes.

"You need to tighten up, man," I say. "Quit frying your brain when you've got a d-spot to look after."

A silent tear runs down the length of his cheek. He falls into my arms, bearhugging me as the sweat from his man tits soaks my T-shirt.

"That was so beautiful, bro! You're a great friend, Johnny. You're more than a friend, you're a brother. God, life is so fucking wonderful!" he wails and starts weeping into my shoulder.

"There, there. You're alright big guy. Everything's gonna be just fine," I whisper as we rock back and forth, holding each other tenderly like two lovers in a hammock.

As he cries it out, I see a green minivan pull to a stop across the street. The doors open and four men with shaggy blonde hair pile out.

"Alright, get it together," I say to Brendan. "You got customers."

He sniffles and wipes his eyes.

"I didn't have anyone coming over today."

I freeze, looking back at the men across the street. I see the white lettering emblazoned across their blue bulletproof vests. P-O-L-I-C-E. It's a raid — and on a Sunday, no less.

"Buddy... cops, cops," I shove Brendan off of me —"It's the fucking cops!"

Screaming like a bitch now, he leaps over the balcony and sprints toward the back of his house. I duck into my own house and lock the deadbolt. In about thirty seconds we'll know who they've got the warrant for — a 50/50 shot. Straight to my room to grab the work, I hear the pigs surrounding the compound, grunting and sniffling like they know it's feeding time.

My hands are shaking as I dump twenty-eight grams of Hector's product into the toilet. I've learned my lesson from the last invasion and started keeping the bulk of my money and dope at a secret stash house away from my permanent residence. It's only by accident that I've still got some unsold stuff on me now, but I was planning on moving it later today. Got caught with my pants down again, but who the fuck raids on a Sunday?

Then it begins — the pounding on the front door. So, it's me they're after? God only knows who's snitching. I flush hard, but like a good shit, some of the dope doesn't want to go down. Fish are floating around the toilet water now. I plunge furiously.

"Fucking mother's cunt!" I scream.

The final grams disappear down the mouth of the commode. Any minute now, that door will come flying off the handle. I wrap last night's haul — about two Gs — into a leftover coke baggie, then bury it inside a fresh jar of mayonnaise and put it back in the refrigerator.

I'm ready for you now, boys. I unlock the door.

"Come in! It's open!" I yell through the window. I kiss the ground with my hands on my head —won't be having no accidents today.

"Don't move!" the first one through the door yells.

"Where am I gonna go?" I mumble into the carpet. Coppers are so dull.

A pack of them are in the house now. Dark sunglasses and long blonde ponytails, they're like Dog the Bounty Hunter's grown cum.

"Where's the dope at?" the leader grunts. Cops always want you to do their job for them.

They cuff me and sit me up on the couch, shooting me their best rap while they tear the house apart. Boilerplate hogwash: How much was I pushing? Was I getting it from Brendan or someone else? We'll be here all night if we have to. Tell us everything now, and we promise you won't spend a minute in jail. But already know I won't, fellas.

I play aghast.

"Cocaine? No way, officers! Never even tried it."

Bullshit so good I could've run for office. I even volunteer to assist in the search.

"Check the bathroom," I say. "Maybe somebody left some in there without me knowing. I have a lot of parties."

I can hear the air deflate from their swollen chests like beach volleyballs — guilty men don't play it this cool. Time to wrap it up, fellas. Your boy is squeaky.

I peek through the blinds, and see Brendan being led away in bracelets to an awaiting squad car. They'd had a warrant for his house, too. Unfortunately, he's not so squeaky — a pile of cash and a bag of Hector's powder are splayed out on the hood of the cops' minivan.

He was slipping alright. For months I'd warned him against bringing customers into his house, especially when he started wholesaling some of his work to other dealers. Almost without a doubt, one of these dealers had gotten pinched and decided to roll on him. How the cops got a warrant to search my house too is a mystery. Perhaps they'd staked me out on surveillance with Brendan. Doesn't really matter now — their case is DOA.

"Alright asshole, stand up," one of them grumbles, and then uncuffs me.

The pigs storm out of the house one by one, nothing but their dicks in their hands.

They'd left my place in shambles, furniture overturned and shelves emptied out all over the floor — but I could give two fucks. I'd beaten them. An ounce of pure Fish to the noggin can't come close to this high.

It wasn't just the four overgrown savages who'd stormed my house that day. It was the judge and the courts, backed by the full approval of the citizenry, who'd granted it. They'd tried to stop me and failed. I felt like I could fly.

"Hector, soy John, del norte. Tenemos un pedo grandísimo juey."

The sun is setting as the last of the coppers drive away.

"We got hit," I say over the burner phone. "The cops got Brendan."

Silence on the other end, and then Hector's mousey voice comes through.

"ya me llamó, dice que quiere dos ladrillos."

So, the singing had begun. Not in custody more than three hours and Brendan had already cracked. Freaked out of his mind and still high on acid, I'm sure it didn't take much to awaken the pigeon in him. The cops had gotten him to phone up Hector and order two kilos. It would make a nice little collar for the DEA, no doubt — maybe they'd even follow the trail all the way back to Mexico. I always knew Brendan was weak, and that in a jam he'd choose self-preservation over honor. But then again, so would most people. I'm just lucky to have dodged the dragnet.

"Gracias," Hector says softly, and hangs up.

I tried calling him a few days later, but the number was disconnected. Some thanks I get for keeping his ass outta jail.

And so, there goes my connection to the raw Fish. Oh well, perhaps it's high time I throw it back to the sea. I'd gotten what I needed from it, setting CJ and I up to expand on the game we know best. But boy, I tell ya — there's no business like snow business, and I ain't never lied.

Salvatore

Dawn breaking over the plains of *Provincia de Santa Fe* is like watching a portrait. I'm pressed against the glass, smoking a Lucky Strike and gazing out onto the *Río Paraná* as the earth rouses from its slumber. My own body is begging for sleep, but the joy in my brain won't allow it. You may never have this moment again. I want a beer *pero se acabó* hours ago. I'd like a hump but the *putas* have retired for the evening. They'd been perfectly lovely, even if they had made me wear a bag. Those were the days when I could screw with a hat on and still make a cummer.

I turn to Sal, sawing logs on the couch with nothing but his socks on. Boy, we shook it up good last night. First, a goodbye dinner with the students from the International School, then bar-crawling all over town, until all we could do was crawl — straight to our preferred skin shack, *La Rosa* — where I'd doled out good American currency for a pair of thoroughbreds to follow us back to my place, a cozy one-bedroom with floor-to-ceiling windows on the thirtieth floor of a high-rise in downtown *Rosario* . I'd say those gals made some of the easiest money they'll ever make in the butt business — two tepid Gringo cocks thrusting uselessly and painlessly under the safe cover of latex — a hooker's free lunch.

Those four months in Argentina are the closest I'll come to heaven. What a cruel, awful place the world is that most will never get to enjoy it with me. Every day, every hour, every minute — I caught a different buzz. And just imagine, it had all been a fluke.

After the cops blitzed and took Brendan to jail, I'd been left with no dope to sell — and, as it turned out, not enough credits to graduate the following spring. I was all set to drop out —school had always been a sideshow to this hustling shit, anyway — but then CJ called me from Spain to tell me how easy it was to study abroad.

"Basically, you just get drunk and take field trips. As long as you don't kill anyone, they'll pass you. Also, Latin chicks love to fuck."

Fine, I'll give it a look-see. Fall of '07, I rented a condo and stashed $40,000 in a safe for CJ to keep the business running in my stead, then I embarked for South America.

Together with my Guinea comrade Salvatore Marzio, a sauce-monkey from New Jersey I'd met the first day at the International School, I'd bathed in the tub of freedom only money and youth can permit. We traversed the land, seeing and doing and drinking and snorting and humping — living, as it were. For the first time in years, I looked to the future and a life without the Trap.

But fate wouldn't have it. Watching the sun climbing up the horizon now, I recall the conversation we had last night — the one that would change my life forever.

"I'm gonna miss you pal," I said, smacking his cheek gingerly — the way I'd seen Italians in movies do it.

"Fucking homo," he chuckled.

When I first met Sal, he was about as refined as a three-day old bag of dog shit. A blue-eyed Dago from South Jersey — where the only way out is a tour of duty or a prison stretch — his time in Argentina had turned him into a man of the world.

The house lights dimmed devil red, smoke in the air so thick you could slice it with a razor. Whores strutted around like peacocks at the zoo, pecking at any trick who smelled like a few *pesos* . They came to *La Rosa* from all over the province on Saturday nights, hoping to harpoon a whale big enough to give them the next six off. It might just be us — our last weekend in Argentina, and our balls were full and our mood merry.

"Fuck it, I retire. Too much stress for a thousand a week," I said, flicking the ash from my Lucky Strike. The music faded and a bright spotlight illuminated the stage.

"You're just saying that cause you're only making a thousand a week," said Sal, before putting down another Fernet and Coke. The guy can drink twenty of those fucking things and still form words. "Kibbles and bits my friend."

"It took me four years to start making those kibbles and bits," I replied. "Besides, the price is too low, and every year the market gets more and more flooded."

I drained my Fernet and ordered two more. Sal turned to me, his jasmine eyes dazzling like Caribbean emeralds.

"Maybe it's time you start looking for new markets," he winked and lighted a cigarette.

The nuns entered stage right. Shuffling forward single file, they kept their heads bowed — solemn, dignified — each one holding out a small candle.

"You mean Jersey? Who's gonna move my product for me — you?" I laughed aloud — a mocking, challenging laugh.

"Don't doubt it, cocksucker," he said. "You know I'm connected."

"The dope game is a lot different than the garbage business, Sally."

Ominous, God-fearing music began pulsating through the club. It was the bone chilling score from the end of *Requiem for a Dream* , when everyone is spun out on smack and the jail surgeon is sawing Jared Leto's arm off.

"Besides," I said. "Moving it across state lines is federal shit. Takes resources, capital — and I blew most of that on this trip buying booze and broads."

"Whose fault is that?"

"Ours," I said. We laughed heartily.

The nuns came to a halt, turning in unison to face the audience. Heads still bowed, they swayed gently back and forth. The satanic music was growing louder. This was my favorite part.

"Thing is Johnny — you don't have any other choice," Sal screamed in my ear.

"What?" I yelled back.

The music reached a fever pitch. The walls were sweating, the tension unbearable. It's as if God and the Devil were at war for our souls. God didn't stand a chance.

The beat dropped — it was Michael Jackson's *Thriller*, right on time. The nuns ditched their candles and shed their outfits, nothing on underneath but birthday meat. Dark nipples, fat asses — smooth, flawless cunts. One of them grabbed the pole, the other a cream-colored twelve-inch. These hoes were born for the stage.

"You're working on borrowed time," Sal continued. "In a few years, weed will be legal — and then you'll be out of a job."

"I know that, Sal."

Just inches from our face, two nuns shared a double-sided plastic sword, engulfing it back and forth like lumberjacks sawing down a tree. They'll need confession tomorrow. If church had been this fun growing up I might have stayed a Catholic.

"You know what a pound of your stuff could sell for on the East Coast?"

"I dunno Sal, how much?"

I was barely listening, transfixed as I was by this young wench curled into a U-shape in front of me, intent on displaying the anatomy of her snapper.

"Thirty-eight, at wholesale."

For a split second I sobered up, and suddenly this gal's gynecology lesson lost its import. I turned to Sal, squinting to see him through my blurry Fernet eyes. At $3,800, I could achieve a profit margin of $1,500 per pound — almost ten times what I could make selling at wholesale in Eugene. Even in my belligerent state, I grasped the implications immediately. This could make me rich.

"Fuck off," I said, hiccupping. "You're full of shit."

"You're right," he said. "The market rate is thirty-eight, but the price to me is thirty-five. That way I'll have them sold before they even arrive."

The nerve of this guy! Already asking for a price break — these goddamn Guineas really make me laugh.

In the corner, a group of curly haired Argie men, apparently celebrating a bachelor party, waived over one of the nuns. The good sister promptly sprinted to the corner of the stage, sliding cunt-first into their eager jowls like a runner at home plate. She moved from one head to the next, letting the animals take turns gnawing hungrily on her cat.

"Okay, kingpin," I said to Sal. "Let's assume you CAN move my bricks — how am I supposed to get them all the way to Jersey? I can't drive across the country every week."

"That's your problem," he said, sprinkling a dollop of Fishscale onto his pinky and blowing it up his nose. "But once you figure it out, you've got a partner on the other end."

The bachelor, a fresh-faced fellow, was powerfully drunk and drowning in nun cunt, his arms flailing helplessly as she jammed his head into her cervix. Shouts and whistles of delight erupted from the crowd.

"I'll run it by CJ when I get back," I said, finishing off my Fernet. "But I doubt he'll go for it. We worked too hard to get back on our feet, and if those pounds get lost in transit it'll put us out of business."

"I got news for you guys," Sal said, sliding the baggie of snort in front of me. "One way or another, you're going out of business. Only thing you get to decide is if you wanna go out rich."

Three of the nuns were pulling the bachelor up on stage. He was in for it alright. They strapped him down to a chair and prepared him for coitus. Dick out, rubber on — it was as if he was being swallowed by naked Argie flesh. The excitement was feverish — tables got knocked over, and in the back of the room, a fight broke out.

"This is your last chance to hit it big," he said, pounding the table. "You'd be stupid to pass it up."

I grinned. Heard that one before.

The trio was fucking him rotten. One rode his face, the other his prick, while the third played rover — transitioning between ass-eating and ball-gobbling and taint-licking. The noise in the place was deafening — you'd have thought we were at a Roman Gladiator match the way the crowd roared.

I ordered two shots of Fernet — one for me and one for Sal.

We raised our glasses.

"To you, Sally."

"And to you, Johnny, the once and future king."

Then, we turned to our new friend on stage, getting plowed so hard his body had gone limp.

"And may his marriage be a long and happy one."

"*Salud.*"

It's all coming back to me now, clarity pushing away the clouds of poison fogging my wet brain like the sun ascending over the steppes of *Santa Fe*.

I finish my Lucky Strike, then I turn to look at Sal, still snoring on the couch. His words ricochet through my brain like a bullet from a .22 pistol.

"The only thing you get to decide is if you wanna go out rich."

Graduation

I hate K-9s, always sticking their snouts where they don't belong. Music to my ears when I hear of one getting put down on the job. From hunting runaway slaves to attacking civil rights marchers to acting as the slobbering henchman in the war on drugs, K-9s have always been on the wrong side of history. The K-9 is my enemy — only difference between him and the man holding his leash are two extra legs. Hope he doesn't choose to come sniffing now. If so, he's in for a pleasant surprise – thirteen bricks of high-powered bubble gum sativa nestled in the lining of my trunk, wrapped tight but not tight enough.

Pissing rain is usually the safest weather to make the trip — keeps the State Troops cozied up in their cruisers with the heat blasting, sipping gas station coffee and getting a suck from a truck stop hooker.

So why the red-and-blue all of a sudden? Could be the Vice trying to make it look like a routine traffic stop. If he brings the K-9 out right away, I'll know I'm done for.

No time to think — only react. Vision narrows, hands go numb, breath ceases and heart beats pound my ear drums like a techno concert. I've got all of five seconds to show him I'm a civilian — a good boy — a tax-paying citizen caught up in a torrential downpour. Somewhere in America right now, there's a guy getting pulled over with sixty pounds of heroin stashed in the panels of his U-Haul truck. This ain't shit.

I see the bucket hat approaching the window, no K-9 with him. A good start.

"Hi there," I offer in my best Leave-It-To-Beaver. "Was I going too fast?"

A pre-emptive confession, cops love it when you tell on yourself. Rain is hitting me in the face through the open window.

"You were going too slow!" he chuckles.

He's a middle-aged white man with cracking skin, one of Nixon's "silent majority," the one for whom Donny promises a return to the glory years of the Empire. Surely, this man sees us as members of the same team, not the bitter enemies that I know we are.

"I was trying to pass you in the fast lane," he continues. "Next time someone comes up behind you, stead'a speeding up, get over and let 'em by."

Silly me. This peace officer is looking out for my safety, is all. I hand him my license and registration.

"Where ya headed?"

"Portland."

He jogs back to his car and hops in. Minutes later, he returns.

"This car is registered to a Mister Charles Jerome?"

"Yes sir, he's my roommate. He let me borrow it for the weekend."

"Long way from home ain't ya?"

Cold sweat forming now, it means trouble when a copper starts to think. He peers over my shoulder into the backseat, then takes a step back and analyzes the vehicle, as though something's not quite right. These pigs and their wild imaginations.

"Where'd you say you were coming from?"

"Ashland, sir."

"What's in Ashland?"

"My girlfriend, sir. Wanted to say goodbye before I ship off to basic training tomorrow."

His narrow eyes widen as suspicion turns to respect. This young man is volunteering to serve his country.

Rain coming down harder now, he hands me back my license and chucks up a quick salute.

"Good luck, son!"

Why, thank you, officer. Now if you don't mind, I'll be getting back to my paper route.

"How was the drive?" CJ asks me as I pull safely into town hours later.

"Smooth as ever," I say. And then, we get to work.

Summer '08. Graduation Day.

The house of cards is in a freefall: the Dow Jones swan dives, the S&P plummets, the masters of mankind are running to the suits in the Big House begging for alms, and our peers can't get a fucking job.

"Ten percent unemployment, they're saying," CJ mumbles, holding a blunt between his teeth.

"Fuck, you made me lose count again."

The room is silent except for the soft pattering of cash hitting the table. I turn up CNN. The talking heads are having a field day alright — Wall Street versus Main Street and subprime mortgages and layoffs and capitalism's crisis of faith. All matters that don't concern us.

"We're the only real capitalists left," I tell CJ, snatching the blunt from his mouth. "Do you see it now?"

We pause to admire the poker table covered in loose bills, the haul from our last shipment. While an entire generation drowns in quicksand waiting tables and living at home with their parents, we're perched aloof in our yuppie downtown loft, safely out of reach from the carnage below.

"Do you see why we do this shit?"

"Money, it looks like," CJ says. "And for me at least, pussy — one day you might get some of that too if you're lucky."

I grin at my partner in crime, exhaling a billowing smoke cloud from the steaming L.

"Because, FUCK THE WORLD, CJ — that's why."

It's the only thing I've ever been certain of.

But times change, and things fall apart. Spring of '09, and the citizens of Oregon are growing restless, chanting heresy about legalizing the sticky herb and wresting it from the hands of "the drug barons who profiteer from its prohibition." Goddamn hippies, don't they know they're fucking with the indelible laws of the Trap? In this forbidden dance of dope, the cops and the pushers are lovers clutched tight in each other's arms, rocking gently back and forth while the junkies keep the music playing. To fuck with this arrangement is to tip the balance of the Earth's axis — to pull back the curtain of the greatest lie told to the American people in a century. This dance — these laws of prohibition — is job security, ensuring dope boys like me stay in business so the coppers still have somebody to chase down.

But by now, it's evident that the countdown to our extinction has begun. More and more legally grown, indoor medicinal weed is flooding the black market by the month, making the price of our outdoor product tick downward. The shipments are taking longer to move, and we've even been forced to start retailing some of our product in order to make payroll.

"The hell's keeping you two?" Kenny asked me over the phone one day.

He's feeling the squeeze, too, as wholesalers like CJ and I demand lower and lower prices for each of his pounds.

It was a race against the clock.

"The end is coming," I tell CJ one summer afternoon as we lounge on our balcony, drinking beer and slapping dominoes. "We need to graduate, or we might as well quit right now."

It's been over a year since I made the Jersey connection with Sal, but when I first proposed the idea to CJ, he vetoed it.

"That's how empires get destroyed," he'd said. "When they reach for too much territory."

"You want to get destroyed or go obsolete? Cause one way or another we're going out of business. Only thing we get to decide is if we want to go out rich."

He didn't bite.

But now, a year later, it's crunch time.

"Sal is ready with the buy-money on the other end," I tell him. "All we need to do is get him the merchandise."

CJ smiles and shakes his head, finishing off his beer.

"Thinking big has never been your problem, Johnny, that's for sure. Just remember, all you ever wanted is what you have now."

"I know that, that's why I have to protect it."

"Very well," he says. "I'm out."

"You're out?"

He nods. "That's what you want, right?"

It's true. He's had one foot out the door for a while now, and there can be no half-stepping on the path I'm headed. It's the smart move — CJ was always smarter. He'd taken all the streets had had to give, leaving the game without so much as a scratch. He had a down payment on a new house, a nice girl, and a bank roll that outta transition him comfortably to the square life.

I'm not sure he even realized how he'd just beaten the devil at his own game, managing to shake himself free of greed's lasso and do what few in the history of mankind have been able to achieve. Instead of "How can I make more?" this man tipped his hat and said, "Thanks, but I've got enough."

That night, I gave him ten thousand dollars as a severance pay. Ten thousand for a lifetime — a pittance compared to what's coming.

"Hello?" the sleepy-eyed Ginzo mumbles in the throng of sleep. I can practically smell the Fernet through the phone.

"Wake your ass up," I say. "Time to get to work."

Part II

THE CLOUDS

2008-2010

ATM

This can't be real, can it? This ATM machine that's fallen at my feet. Reminds me of that African Parable where the warrior shoots an arrow into the recalcitrant raincloud, showering the drought-plagued land and injecting new life into the village below.

This wasn't supposed to happen — not to a hapless sack like me. Whole life's been mired in mediocrity. Never won nothing, always content with second best, indoctrinated by the putrid middle-class mentality of Europeans who'd long ago accepted their lot — happy as they were to be off the farm and into the cubicle. So many generations removed from the swamp, yet we own not a single piece of land save for the house I grew up in. So much education yet we act stupid, slogging our way through a morning commute on the way to work for the next motherfucker, falling for the dangle of the carrot instead of nurturing our own garden. Nothing to pass onto our heirs but some scraps and the insanity of our genetics, and then watch as the cycle goes round. All that ends now, with me.

I wasn't supposed to get this far — in the days of the Trap, many tried their hand, but few emerged with anything to show for it but gas money and some free weed to smoke. I had no capital, no criminal connections, no army of killers by my side, and certainly no mentors to lead the way. Yet here I stand, in arm's reach of a million untraceable dollars — a drug dealer's dream. The American Dream.

Sal kept his word alright. The dunce — who one drunken Rosario night got his favorite Argentine beer brand tattooed onto one of his ass cheeks — has shaped up to be an astute business partner. He's turned South Jersey into the U.S. Mint, printing fucking cash. The plan to undercut worked. At $3,500, he can wholesale them five at a time. He has dealers driving in from Philly, Delaware — even some Dominicans from Washington Heights who make the three-hour pilgrimage south to Camden each week to re-up on our work.

"All's you gotta do is keep it coming in," he reminds me daily, as if I'd forgotten.

Things have changed on my end — I had to tighten up. I'm a factor now, doing big numbers, and my racket would make for a nice little boost on a police stat sheet. No more touching the work, now it's my courier making the weekly drive down to Southern Oregon to visit Kenny and Walt. This recession is good for business — motivates a nice God-fearing kid to take chances he otherwise wouldn't, like risking Fed time for $300 round trip.

As soon as my courier returns safely to base, we unload the merchandise at his girlfriend's apartment, a cozy top floor walk-up sitting kitty corner to the northeast police precinct.

Next, we prepare the birds to take flight. The methods of moving work across the country are no different than any company or product. By land or air are the options, and are switched up depending on the size and speed of the order. If Sal demands twenty units, we might send them five-day delivery in a portable shipping container stuffed inside some old couches. For smaller orders, our bread and butter is overnight Federal Express. The money returns the same way, but always the opposite of how the work was shipped. So, if I send the merchandise by air, I insist my money be shipped back to me by ground, and vice versa.

Size is our greatest advantage — miniscule. The breadth and volume of commerce zig-zagging the United States at all times is astounding, almost incomprehensible. A hundred million packages a day between the big three — not to mention hundreds of thousands of freight trucks transporting untold billions worth of cargo. It is amongst this madness that my humble wares quietly and conveniently blend in with the sauce.

Today, we're going into surgery. It's exacting work, and I spare no precaution. Ten pounds of Banana Kush reeks wonderfully and sticks to everything, and even the slightest contact with anything outside of the vacuum-sealed bag can compromise an entire package.

"Gloves," I say to my courier-turned-surgeon's assistant.

I run through four pair of surgical gloves for every one box. I take the first unit and cut open the top of the bag. I then start transferring weed by the handfuls from its original bag to a vacuum-sealed one. I pass it to my assistant, who wipes it down with a laundry strip. I change gloves, take the food-savor bag and run it through a vacuum sealer machine until it is sealed shut. My assistant will check the sealed bag for any rips or tears, then once that's clear, we'll put another bag over it and run that through the sealer one more time.

We repeat this process ten times, once for every pound being shipped. Now that each unit has been vacuum-sealed and is completely odorless, it's time to pack them for their trip. We line two medium-sized FedEx shipping boxes with bubble foam, then arrange five pounds one by one inside of each box. Finally, we layer the boxes with one more sheet of foam and then tape the boxes shut. The entire process takes us two hours.

Cue the broad. My courier's girlfriend emerges dressed in a business suit and high heels. I need someone presentable dropping the packages off at the Fed Ex store. That narcotics routinely get smuggled through the mail is common knowledge in the parcel industry, and I don't want to give the guy behind the counter with the gauges in his ears making $10 an hour any reason to believe it might be worth rifling through our boxes before they get shipped off.

Lastly, I stick the shipping labels with the two Jersey addresses onto their respective boxes. Sal rotates through five or six different safe houses used for receiving the merchandise, and the same goes for my end.

As added precaution, I've created fake companies with phony return addresses to mark on the shipping labels.

My courier helps his girlfriend carry the boxes to her awaiting car idling out back. I peel off two hundred-dollar bills and hand them to her.

"Drive safe," I smile.

"Yeah, yeah," she rolls her eyes and snatches the bills.

Now they're off. Less than twenty-four hours from now, my product will be getting broken down and bagged up by a couple of Guinea hoods in a Camden basement. What a time to be alive.

I take out the bat phone and text Sal with the tracking numbers, then go online to check the progress of my money, arriving tomorrow via Fed Ex Ground Delivery.

Through the night and into the following morning, I check the tracking compulsively.

"We call it GO, cause when you got it, it's a green light, but when you don't — shit, you're stuck on red."

Sweet Tea's words of street wisdom are still embedded in me after all these years. Indeed, cash is the coal keeping the fires of our locomotive fed. Lost product is easily replaced, but money lost can wipe us out faster than the Spanish Flu. Already, we've had two packages stuffed with over $40,000 lifted from us by some lucky mail carriers, who'll now be retiring a year early.

"Wrap my money like I wrap your weed!" I'd admonished Sal one day, after a package of cash turned up empty at my doorstep.

But today, the eagle has landed safely. I text my courier — he's got one last errand to run. An hour later, he's sliding the package under my door. I'm a ghost alright. The only people who know where I sleep are him, CJ, and the occasional whore.

I get a text from Sal — the work has just arrived on his end, thus completing another seamless transaction. Historians of the Trap will argue over who the bigger kingpin was — Pablo Escobar or El Chapo — when in reality, Federal Express has delivered more drugs than those two combined.

And now, for the payoff.

Counting money is a spiritual experience. The deadbolt latches, the shades get drawn, and the lights go dim. I open the Fed Ex envelope and remove the small rectangle box stuffed inside. Wrapped in layers of duct tape, I tear away at the box like a diabetic trying to get at a piece of candy. I'm almost there now, I can smell it. Dirty cash has a unique, damp odor — a hint of ink, a trace of marijuana, a touch of cocaine, and the sweat of a million anonymous hands it's had to pass through in order for us to finally be together. You can rest now, my love. You're safe with me.

I lay them out side by side on the coffee table in front of me — thirty-five stacks of a thousand dollars each, bound together by rubber bands. I'm all set to pray, when I'm interrupted by a phone call — the most beautiful voice in the world is on the other end.

"Is that my Grandson?"

"Papa!"

"When the hell are you coming to see me?"

"Soon, Papa, soon. I promise. Just been busy with work."

"Your mother tells me you're running some sort of business now?"

"Yeah, Papa — it's kind of like ... a courier service. We deliver packages for people."

"That's fantastic. And how's everything going?"

"I made eighty thousand dollars last month."

"Son of a bitch! That's alright, now isn't it?!"

"It's amazing what I've stumbled into Papa. It must be like when you found oil in Alberta."

"Yeah, that was quite a time alright —'till the Feds came and took it all from me. Oh well, that's life, isn't it?"

"I'd like to avoid that part, Papa."

Papa is my hero, see. My mother's father, born to Scottish peasants who immigrated to the frozen tundra of Alberta. With only a high school education, he managed to leverage the Canadian oil boom into a multi-million-dollar conglomerate. A betting man, he overplayed his hand one too many times and went belly up, but not before passing his fitful genes onto his eldest grandson. My mother always used to worry about how he and I were so similar, but lucky for her I won't repeat his mistakes.

"Listen to me John," he coughs. "I'm dying."

"Don't say that."

"What? You'd rather I bullshit you? You spend your whole life bullshitting people, the least a dying man deserves is the right to be honest."

"I know, Papa. I'm sorry. I'm just scared, is all."

"Don't be, cause I'm not. A man is only scared of death when he knows he hasn't lived right — never forget that. Whatever matters to you in life, that's all that matters. Do it until there's nothing left."

"I want to do it my way Papa, that's all. And I'm doing it. They can control everyone else, but they don't control me."

This makes him chuckle.

"We're a lot alike, me and you. Since the day you were born, I could see it in your eye. You were cut from a different cloth. It's not easy, this way we live. But there ain't much other choice."

"I love you, Papa," I say, biting my lip. He didn't say it back, but that's okay — he never was much good with feelings no how.

"I'm gonna lie down for a nap. You come visit me soon, you hear?"

"I will, Papa."

I hang up, wiping the water from my eyes.

I turn back to the mission at hand. I say a quick prayer for Papa, and then I begin to count.

One, two, three, four, five. I count for those who came before me — for my ancestors, the children of the wretched, who existed only in hardship and toil. I count for my Papa, who through gritted teeth managed to pull himself up out of the slime, only to lose it all. This money is reparations Papa. I wish I could crawl into the grave and share it with you. Count, count, count, count. I finish counting and then I count again. I count because this is what's coming to me. I count because someone has to do it — someone has to set the table so future generations can eat. No different from Grandpa Roosevelt flooding Hong Kong's shores with Opium, or Joe Kennedy moving Prohibition molasses from Cuba to the harbors of South Boston, or my own Papa extracting black gold from the frigid soil when others said it couldn't be done. I count, count, count, count. I count for me. I count because life is pain and money is morphine. I didn't choose to be here — I was tossed into this grief, and now money is payback for all the years spent in suffering. I count because I'm a dope sick junkie and this needle shot of cash brings me respite. I count because all of us are prisoners here on earth, but with this money — for a moment at least — I am free. Count, count, count, count, and then I count once more.

I pick up the phone and text Sal: "You're twenty dollars short."

Filthy

This game is a motherfucker — do I have to scream it at you? The minute you think you've got her on cruise control is the minute she hits an ice slick and barrels toward the cliff's edge.

"The only problem is what to do with all the fucking cash !" I hear Frank Lopez say to Tony in the background. It's a bigger problem than I thought, Frank.

"Mama!" I yell to the boss in the other room. "Did you see my computer bag?"

"John? Is that you?" the elegant but aging lady is still in her bathrobe, delightfully surprised by her firstborn who rarely comes to visit anymore.

"Mama, did you see my old computer bag? I put it under the sink yesterday."

"Why the hell would you do a thing like that for?"

Because I've got too much money, Mama. I've got too much of it, and I don't know where to put it all. Some of it is buried in your garden, some is stashed in the attic, a few hundred thousand is scattered in various safe deposit boxes throughout the city, and the rest sits atrophying in storage units, shoeboxes, and the safe next to my bed. Haven't had a good night's sleep on that thing in awhile — terrified as I am of losing it all and rejoining the ranks of the peasants.

"Have you seen it or not?"

She shoves past me and starts tidying up the bathroom that needs no tidying. "You mean that old ripped bag? I threw it out yesterday, there was a bunch of holes in it anyway—"

Before she can finish, I'm out the door and sprinting down the stairs. Garbage day was when?

I poke my head out the back door — thought so. The garbage truck is roaring down the street away from our house, leaving behind two empty trash cans in the driveway.

"Is everything alright honey?" Mama comes lumbering down the stairs after me. "Was there something in that bag?"

Fifty thousand in cash, is all. Must've weighed a few pounds at least, funny you didn't bother looking inside, but you've always been one to mind your own business. I'd wrapped it in duct tape and stashed it under your sink for a few days, just till I found a better place to put it. Now the garbage man's annual salary is in the back of his truck, heading to the landfill where it'll drown in an ocean of dirty diapers and eggshells and coffee grounds and used condoms.

My legs start to wobble and I feel this morning's breakfast rising in my throat. I steady myself on the kitchen table, sweat leaking through my pores like tailpipe oil. Breathe, big fella, just breathe — you'll make it back in a week.

I turn to Mama and force my lips into the shape of a smile.

"It was nothing Mama, just some papers and stuff. Let's have coffee."

A dope dealer's dilemma alright. True, most never make it far enough to have this problem. I remember a time when I could only dream of having too much cash to hide. Now here I am, entering the third and final phase of this yellow-brick-road to riches — the rinse cycle.

Time to shower off this filth. I know someone who might be able to help.

Colombia

Love the sea, always have. Terrifying but thrilling, it's like a planet within a planet, a graveyard of secrets as vast as the depths of space.

Should've been a buccaneer, really. Had I not been born half-a-millennia too late, I'm certain I would have commandeered a fleet of outlaw ships — exploring the high seas, bartering silk and spices and tobacco, impregnating indigenous women, and running from the Queen's Navy.

Dope dealers are pirates of the modern era — the mercantile class, the middlemen — utilizing capital and technology to subvert the kingdom and its laws to deliver from point A to B the world's forbidden booty.

Fitting then, that I should find myself here, in Colombia — land of the pirates.

The baby blue Caribbean waves collide gently against the cliffside. From the villa, I can look down and see the entire town of *Taganga* lying at my feet, like a Lord admiring his fiefdom. Just a fishing village really, untouched by time — save for the blonde-haired beasts from Europe and Oceania spilling in by the busload.

Colombia has changed, they say. Been fifteen years since Medellin and Cali went bust and Pablo got his bullet. Now, they're calling it paradise, and *Taganga* its best kept secret. Not for long. Every day, more and more pink-skinned Norseman with hungry noses and horny dicks wash up on her shores like the second coming of *Christo Colombo*.

"'Cha looking at?" Sal drapes his arm over my shoulder.

He's let Wesley Snipes from *New Jack City* dress him today — a purple suit, gold pinky ring, dark designer shades, and a cross dangling from his neck.

"It's these Europeans — fucking animals, every last one of them."

"Animals with deep pockets, my friend," he brings the key with the tiny white mountain up to his nostril and makes it vanish up his septum. "Didn't I tell you this place was heaven? Fuck Argentina. I mean, I love it — don't get me wrong — but THIS fucking place?! This is everything we talked about!"

"You sure about this guy?" I'm sweating from nerves and the humidity.

"Hey, what are you worried about? I told you, he's been vetted. He works with my cousin Nicky's uncle, the Mob guy from Newark. They say he's the best."

"Yeah, yeah. Everything's the best with you Meatballs."

"There he is," Sal says. "Do me a favor, try not to be a jerk off for an hour. If that's possible."

"Amigos!" the man greets us with a disarming smile, like we're old friends.

We've found a player alright. Dawning aviator shades and a thousand-dollar suit with the top buttons comfortably undone, he looks like a Latin George Clooney.

"I am Andres. Welcome to Colombia. What do you think of your new investment?"

He takes a step back to let us admire the manor — a three story Spanish colonial with seven oversized bedrooms, two balconies, an infinity pool with a jacuzzi, and a rooftop deck with a 360-degree view as far as the eye can see.

"Not bad," I say. "Why are they selling?"

"The owner passed away, I'm afraid, in a terrible accident. Fortunately for us, before his death he'd fallen into some debt. Now that debt is being passed along to his family, which means they'll be willing to sell to us at a bargain."

This guy is too slick, but I suppose in his line of work that's a requirement. Andres has the most dangerous job in the drug business, entrusted with the fortunes of men powerful enough to reach out and touch him no matter what corner of the globe he hides. He and his kind are indispensable — the link to the legitimate world inaccessible to the marooned outlaw operating in the shadows.

Just like trafficking, money laundering is a team sport. How is it that a kingpin holed-up in a remote Latin American jungle can move hundreds of millions in bulk cash all the way to Europe, to be washed and rung out to dry through a shell company in London, only to emerge on the other end and land safely in a Panamanian bank account? Andres is how. For every gangster with a gold plated .45 tucked into his belt, there is a team of lawyers, accountants, and investment bankers working in tandem to ensure that his money moves safely along the underground railroad of dirty dollars.

That's the very reason for our visit today — to seek the employ of Andres' services.

"You'll be getting in at the perfect time," he continues. "In a few years, Colombia will become like Mexico, and *Taganga* the new *Cancún* ! You could operate it as a hotel or keep it for short-term rentals. I'm telling you, this is THE best piece of property on the whole *Santa Marta* coast. Even if you don't touch it, in five years, the value will go up threefold."

And there it is — a neat little way to clean up some of our filthy presidents' faces.

"Whaddaya say, Johnny? You ready for early retirement or what?" Sal says with a glassy eyed grin, but I barely hear him now. Something more pressing has captured my attention.

I remove my shades — need to be sure it's not the booze and too much sun playing tricks on me.

Walking up behind Andres now, wearing a business skirt and high heels — is the sum of evolution. With white skin tanned a shade darker from generations of conquering, her jet-black mane is long and shiny like a shampoo commercial, her lips full and pouty, and her perfect tits protrude the top of her white button up shirt like a stepmom in a dirty movie. Her legs seem to never end, taut and curvy as they move up, up, up, up, up, up, until finally disappearing beneath her skirt on the road to a hidden treasure I would happily kill to unearth. Struck by a lightning bolt, like Michael upon first laying eyes on Apollonia, her unflinching stare melts my manhood as though I'm made of candle wax.

"John," Sal snaps me back to the present.

I regain a pulse and look at Andres. "What's the price tag?"

"The entire estate is $295,000 – U.S. Plus, another $150,000 for my services."

"That's a big escrow fee," I say. "I could buy another house for that."

"You could, yes. But how do you plan on moving that much money from the U.S. into a Colombian bank account? It's not like the old days — you can't just march up to the teller with a bag of cash. My connections are the only way to ensure your purchase goes through safely and without alerting Colombian or American authorities."

"And how do you plan on doing that?"

"Simple. My company here in Colombia will purchase the property for you, using our own funds. You will deliver the cash — $450,000 in total — to a contact of mine in New York City. Once this is done, we will sign the deed to the property over to you."

I look at my princess. Her expression is unmoved — the same proud, stoic lass I'd fallen in love with. Slowly, she removes the dark shades covering her face. Fuck me! I'm so startled I nearly trip and fall backwards down the side of the cliff. This bitch has a lazy eye! What had been a perfect 10 just two seconds before had now become a solid 7.5. No wonder she's into me. It was like a message from on High, a superbly astute metaphor for my life — just a little off. But it matters not, for I love her just the way she is. With one eye locked on me and the other looking at the sea, she blinked once, deliberately, as though urging me to take the deal.

"I assure you my reputation is impeccable, *Juanito,*" Andres continues, "and my fee competitive."

"Okay, but how do we know you'll transfer the deed once you have the cash? Your word isn't enough, all due respect."

"Hey, relax, will ya?" Sal interjects. "I told you — he's vetted."

I shoot daggers at Sal, who's rubbing the roof of his mouth with his tongue. Need to cool it with the candy, fella.

"Está bien, no hay bronco," Andres chuckles, removing his shades. "I appreciate the way you do business, *parche.* Why don't you leave Sal down here as a guarantee? He'll make sure everything transfers over smoothly once you've brought the cash to my associate in the States. How does that sound to you, Don Salvatore?"

"What, and stay down here an extra two weeks?" Sal says. "Fucking fine by me."

"Good, *temenos un trato entonces?"*

"Fine. You got a deal," I say, shaking his perfectly moisturized hand. Boy, this guy is slick.

"Splendid. I'll have my assistant Maria fill you in on the details. *Maria Fernando, le presento a mis socios nuevos, Salvatore y Juan."*

Maria Fernanda, is it? Maria Fernanda Mitchell — it'll grow on her.

She steps towards me, her stare cutting into my flesh, exposing my soul for the desperate lovesick wretch I've become. Even with one eyeball trying to escape from her head, she is stunning, wild — the apex of femininity.

Clutching in a nervous fart, I extend my hand, but it gets blocked by Sal like he's going in for a rebound.

"The pleasure is all mine, Maria," he says, breathing a cocaine-halitosis cocktail into her face. "Since I'll be staying in town awhile, maybe you can show me around?"

Her eyes drift over his shoulder and settle on me. For the first time in our meeting, she smiles — so perfect I curse my very existence and the God who permitted us to meet, only to have us say goodbye.

She turns back to Sal.

"*A la orden,*" she says gracefully.

"It's settled then," Andres says. "Let's have a toast, shall we?"

Maria fetches the Johnny Walker Blue, a monthly Colombian salary in each gulp. Four scotch glasses clink together in the late afternoon sun, shining down on us like it's ours and ours alone. This deal is a home run — for less than half-a-million bucks, we'll be receiving a palace we can convert into a hotel and watch as the tourists fall over each other trying to give us their money.

I'm entering act three, the final stage of the game: when dirty money mixes with the clean, completing the criminal's evolution from dope boy to legitimate businessman. No longer content with simply being free, my aim is to construct a juggernaut for the future. And now, with the purchase of this hotel, the first stones of my empire had been laid.

Maria

"*This what it's all about, Manny ?*" a sloppy Tony laments to Manolo on the big screen.

It's late, and I feel empty — empty like the champagne bottle and the shrimp platter and the desert tray resting on my bony chest like a pampered Bavarian prince.

Money isn't everything, it's the only thing , an old school cat once said to me. He was one of those wino type heads, used to hang in front of the neighborhood liquor store selling loosies and bumming change so he could cop his jug of Carlos Rossi. *Money isn't everything — it's the only thin g.* Funny coming from a man who never had any — guess that's why he believed in it so much.

"What about the revolution?" I'd asked him once.

He stared at me with eyes that seemed to sag with all of the world's sorrow.

"It got sold," he said. "Now go on and buy me something to drink."

And so it went, I listened to the wino and traded in my ideals for a dope sack. Happiness I may never know, but in the eyes of that broken man — never two nickels to rub together — I witnessed misery. The former I can do without, but the latter I cannot live with.

What's the matter, big fella? Must be getting cold feet. It's first down and inches, but that doesn't quell the unease simmering in my guts. Think I hear something — the night is quiet except for the hissing of the Caribbean wind filling my hotel room. I'm penthouse high in downtown *Cartagena,* goosed after the bumpy four-hour journey from *Taganga.*

After our meeting, Maria escorted Sal to a safe house on the outskirts of town, while I rode with Andres and his bodyguard back to Cartagena. To be sure I didn't have a tail, after they dropped me off at my hotel, I checked out and caught a cab to a different hotel on the other side of the city.

I step through the French doors onto the veranda, naked except for my flip flops. The warm evening breeze blows refreshing gusts of wind against my balls. The sea is pitch black — frighteningly so. It's like a charred inferno swallowing everything in its path as it inches closer towards land. Something isn't sitting right about this whole thing, but I can't pinpoint what it is. Perhaps it's just the seafood platter.

I draw deep on the night air and force myself to smile.

"*It could be worse,*" I hear Manny telling Tony. He's damn right.

Click. A hammer retracts. That steel touch on the back of my head is unmistakable.

"The cash is in the safe," I say in Spanish. "Code is 6969."

That'll never get old.

"Turn around, *puto,*" a mellifluous, feline voice commands.

Hands to the heavens, I slowly turn around. Impossibly more beautiful than when we first met, Maria Fernanda is standing before me, a pearl-handle pistol leveled at my face. She's gripping it with the authority of a killer — controlled, impartial.

"Did you think we wouldn't noticed you changed hotels?" She says, grinning. The lazy eye is excited now, oscillating from the corner of her eye socket to the center and back again, as though mocking me.

"*No se,*" I mutter, breath bated, waiting for the shot to ring out.

"We know everything. Andres would never have agreed to meet with you otherwise."

"Fair enough. But why the gun?"

"In case I have to use it."

"Sounds like you've got it all covered."

I notice she's done her makeup, applied fresh lipstick, and exchanged the business suit for a low-cut yellow lace dress that barely covers her inner thighs.

"Who are you working with?" she says softly. "I'll give you one chance."

"I thought you knew everything?"

"I'd like to hear it from you."

"It's just me and Sal. We're not the Feds. I swear on our future children."

She lets the grin blossom into a smile. Still with the gun pointed at my head, she leans in.

"What makes you think I want kids?"

I'm the one grinning now. Her lips collide with mine, so soft and yummy I could bite them off. Faster and faster, her C cups come out and I'm on them like a baby calf, biting and licking and sucking. She's moaning as I lift up her dress, feeling the heat emanating from beneath her silk thong. Wish I could suspend this moment in time. The best part of coitus is feeling a woman's gash over her underwear for the first time — it's like being a boy on Christmas Day trying to guess what's inside the present before the wrapping paper comes off.

Still on the veranda, she's laid against a recliner with her legs pinned in the air while I slurp up the juices of her precious organ like a Polynesian on a fresh coconut. She's shaking now, but won't let go of the gun. No bother, under pressure is the best way to eat cunt.

I breach her tulip with my long fingers and guide them in and out while I tickle her bell with the tip of my tongue. She's twitching and convulsing like an epileptic, and soon I feel the flood waters breaking the levy. I let the prize dribble off my chin like a child in a watermelon-eating contest.

"*Ya, basta,*" she begs, but I keep up the assault — nobody points a gun at me.

She's on the brink again, shivering despite the warm night air. She covers her mouth with her free hand to stifle the screams, but I knock it away. Scream, *puta* — scream so loud that God himself can hear how much I love you. She's finally had it. Dropping the gun, she throws her head back and howls in ecstasy. I stand up and kick the gun away like I'd seen cops on T.V. do it, then I pull out my own piece.

When the time for climax arrives, I bury my seed as deep inside of her as science will allow. We repeat this again and again, pausing only to let my weapon reload. Finally, I let off the last shot, and we collapse onto the king size bed. *Scarface* is still playing softly in the background. She puts flame to a *porro* — a joint wrapped in THC dust — and passes it to me.

"You must really think you're special, making me cum like that."

"Not special, just studied a lot of game tape."

She rolls her eyes and flicks my shriveled member.

"Do you always carry a gun to your… liaisons?" I ask her.

"I always carry one everywhere. You met the man I work for."

"I thought he was untouchable?"

"*Véngase* , anyone can be touched. This is still Colombia."

"Do you like your line of work?"

She shrugs and puffs the *porro* .

"It pays, if nothing else, and it's my job — whether I like it or not is irrelevant."

"So why not save up and go legit, like me and Sal?"

She giggles, that condescending giggle women do that reduces men to little boys.

"Is that how you think this game ends?"

"It can be, if you're smart and don't get too greedy."

"Greed turns smart men dumb. This country is full of them."

"So, what then? You're just gonna follow them off the cliff?"

"Oh, *cariña* ," she smiles, caressing my cheek. "Perhaps in America you can just walk away, but this is Colombia, and the man I work for won't allow it."

Maria is embroiled alright, but she never really had a choice. Born in a Medellin slum and abandoned at birth, she was adopted by an oligarchic family from the countryside who raised her like an indentured servant. At fifteen, she ran away to Cartagena and lived on the streets for some time, prostituting and begging to keep from starving. She was already blossoming into an awesome beauty, however, which soon afforded her access to Cartagena high society, where she took to reeling in and robbing wealthy tourists and businessmen. One evening at the bar of a popular hotel, she was running her game past a local financial magnate. When he excused himself to go to the bathroom, she spiked his drink, but was spotted by the bartender who alerted the man when he returned.

"You want me to call the cops?" the bartender asked him.

"No, no. I've got a better idea," the man said, grinning at the incredulous young Maria.

That man was Andres, and he hired her on the spot. Starting off as a messenger, Maria eventually got promoted to money courier. Now, she's arranging and sitting in on meetings with his top clients — the leaders of cartels big and small — from Lima to Tijuana to Patterson, New Jersey. Of course, this cushy employment comes at a price. One late night after work at his cliffside mansion, a drunken Andres forced himself on her. When she resisted, he took it.

"I am the hand that feeds you, *puta* , and the one who kept you out of jail," he reminded her.

From time to time, she is obliged to acquiesce his advances.

"But only when his wife is out of town and he's drunk or coked out of his mind," she says.

I sit there listening — dumbstruck. This broad is an open book alright, known her for twelve hours and I'm already getting the autobiography.

"I'm in too deep, *Juan* ," she continues. "I know his organization inside and out — enough to put him and a hundred cartel leaders away for life. He'll never let me go – not alive.

"You're sure there's nothing you can do?"

She shakes her head regrettably, then grabs her gun from the nightstand and points it in the air. She takes aim at the ceiling and pretends to fire off a round.

"Just this," she smirks playfully.

I snatch the gun from her hand and set it down, then I take her in my arms. "Don't talk like that. Let me help you."

"You can't help me," she scoffs, elbowing me off of her.

"Try me."

She grins and re-lights the *porro*.

"Marry me," she says, leaning in and blowing smoke from the *porro* into my mouth.

"Come again?"

"You heard me. I need to get to the States, but the only way I'll get a passport is if I'm married."

"You're serious?"

I'm too high for this shit right now.

She nods. "I'll give you a hundred thousand dollars up front, plus another hundred in five years after I get my U.S. citizenship. I'll also give you two percent of my cut every month from cocaine sales after I take control of the New York market."

"Maria —"

"After I have my citizenship, you can divorce me and walk away. Unless, of course," she leans down and locks my stunned mouth in a deep kiss, "...you've fallen in love with me."

I'm way ahead of her.

Now it's 8 A.M. and we're in the back of a cab on the way to the airport. I've got an early flight to Portland, and I'm due in New York with the cash by next Friday.

My mind is reeling from last night. Marriage? If there's anyone I can make it work with, it's Maria — and that little dowry she's offering is tempting indeed. But what had she meant by taking over the cocaine trade? Was Andres expanding from laundering into trafficking now? I need to sleep. I suddenly miss home and CJ and the days when all we wanted were a few dollars to help us wiggle out of a day job. I dreamt of freedom, but as it turns out, freedom can be very complicated.

"Just think about it," she says as the cab pulls up to my gate. "I might work for bad men, but I'm a woman of my word."

"Ok, I will."

I lean in and kiss her goodbye.

"I love you," I say.

"I love you, too. I'll see you in New York."

Promise

Mozart's symphony, a child's first words — perfect, divine sounds that still can't compare to the rat-tat-tat-tat-tat-tat-tat-tat-tat of dollar bills running through a counting machine. I'm mesmerized, watching as the rectangle sheets topple neatly on top of each other until the stack reaches a thousand, then a rubber band and the flick of a pen on a spreadsheet before it's added to the pile.

Far from being inanimate, each of these bundles contain life. For within every ten, twenty, fifty, and hundred, there is a story — a unique, untraceable saga that begins at the U.S. Mint in Philadelphia and ends in the bank account of a shell company in London's financial district.

From the cradle to the grave, each bill lives a distinct, anonymous existence, like the fingerprints of the billions of anonymous beings it passes through, each with their own anonymous tales of existence, whose only guarantee is the certainty of their death and their need for those rectangle bills.

Some of these beings decided they needed drugs to accompany them on their journey, and so set their bills on the long climb up the invisible mountain until finally they've coalesced at the summit, wrapped in rubber bands and resting on the table here in front of me.

Rat-tat-tat-tat-tat-tat-tat-tat-tat-tat. That's the sound of the locomotive dragging mankind out of the swamp — and that acrid, oily odor emanating off the bills is what's keeping it out. Dirty money, like the cover of *Atlas Shrugged* , is the Herculean Adonis holding up the world on its mighty shoulders. In the wake of the global financial crisis, the banks have fallen on scuffed knees, arms outstretched, begging the barons of Saudi oil and Afghan poppy and Peruvian coca to shower them with liquidity. The gates of the dam have lifted, and now, dark money from every corner of the planet is spilling into Europe by the trillions.

At least, that's what Andres tells me — sure doesn't feel like a transcontinental conspiracy now, sitting in this musty ass office. Rat-tat-tat-tat-tat-tat-tat. That and the ticking clock on the wall are the only noises in the room. A toad-faced Latino man with librarian glasses sits behind a desk, checking the count with the dispassion of a DMV employee. $450,000 in cash, bound by stacks of a thousand, is piled up in front of him. Blue smoke from the Camel resting on his bottom lip swirls around his head like a genie. He coughs violently and lets out a fart.

I turn to Maria seated in the chair next to me. She giggles, then grabs my hand and massages it reassuringly. I'm a nervous wreck, ear cocked for the sound of the Feds, who'll surely come busting through the door any minute now to kidnap my life savings.

Through the office window, I get a perfect view of the city sitting snugly across the Hudson, so bold and beautiful and painted extra pretty in autumn red. Eases my mind alright, the rotten apple, though she's looking a lot riper these days. Spent the last week with Maria hobnobbing around Manhattan, sparing no indulgence — hotel suites, dinners, shows. Even took her to Staten Island so she could ride that fucking ferry. She's worth every moment and every penny, and like New York, every day I discover something new I love about her.

Finally, we received word from Colombia — coast is clear. We'd been in a holding pattern while the bosses did reconnaissance, sending us zig-zagging through the city to be certain we weren't being followed.

Now, we're on the Jersey side of the river in this cluttered office sitting above a used tire shop, giving my filthy money a bath. The man seated behind the desk is called *Sapo*, aptly named for his amphibious face. He is the point man for Andres' operation in America — every cartel dollar passes through his hands before leaving the country.

Since I'm the richer of the duo, I've agreed to put up all the money for the acquisition of the property, with Sal covering the operational expenses until the hotel is up and running. In exchange, I'll get a larger stake of the company, plus points on the back end if and when the hotel gets resold.

"Everything okay down there?" I'd asked him over the phone the other night, laying in the hotel bed next to Maria.

"You kidding me? Fucking perfect. Andres really knows how to host. He put me up in one of his mansions and he sends me a different broad every night."

"Alright, just watch your back."

Sapo snaps the final rubber band around a bill stack and adds it to the pile.

"*Listo pues,*" he says, rubbing his eyeballs wearily.

"*Listo,*" Maria nods.

She takes out her new phone, one of those cutting-edge models they're calling a "smartphone"— basically a computer in your pocket. They're saying it's going to change the world, connecting everyone everywhere at all times. That'll be the death blow for outlaws like me — nowhere left to run or hide.

"The money's all here," she says to Andres. "You can transfer the deed now, *muy bien.*"

She hangs up and turns to me.

"Congratulations, Mr. Mitchell. You've just gone legit."

That afternoon, we're strolling along the Jersey City boardwalk locked into each other's arms like European aristocrats, staring at mighty Manhattan across the river.

"How do you feel?" she asks me.

"Like I won the lottery."

"You did," she says smiling, then smacks my butt playfully. "Have you thought anymore about my proposal?"

"Yes... but what about Andres? What happens when he finds out you fled to the States to be with me?"

"Don't worry about Andres. I spoke to him, and he's agreed to it."

I cock my eyebrow suspiciously.

"Just like that? You're sure?"

"*Sí, mi amor.* He's expanding into distribution, and I convinced him to let me oversee his New York operation."

"Maria," I sigh. "My whole plan is to get out of the game, not go in deeper."

"*No te preocupes,*" she says. "You won't be involved in any way, aside from receiving a portion of the profits. All you have to do is relax and look pretty for me. You'll be my trophy husband."

She's got some strong rap alright, batting her long eyelashes at me knowing damn well I can't refuse them. Either she's playing me or she really does love the kid — maybe both? She did let it be known from jump what her intentions were — that she was in fact using me for citizenship and offering to compensate me handsomely for it. Worst case, I come out of this a rich man with a story to tell, and best case, well, it is standing before me, my crooked-eyed Queen, the most beautiful creature to ever bless my life. Wish I could thank her mother's, mother's, mother's, mother's, mother for bringing her into existence.

"You sure you wanna do this?" I say. "It gets cold here in the winter."

"Well, if it gets too cold we can always visit Colombia. I know of a good hotel in *Taganga* we could stay in," she giggles and bites her lip.

"Fine then. Maria Fernanda Gonzalez —"

"De *Medellin*."

"Right, de *Medellin*. Will you marry —"

But before I can get the words out, she jumps into my arms, kissing and squeezing me like a pet monkey.

"*Sí, mi amor.* I do."

And so, it was settled. For the kid who could never get it right, never hold down a job or make a team, all of the pieces were finally coming together. From dime sacks to pounds to international real estate and a Colombian kingpin fiancé, I was one of the fortunate few of my generation to seize the time and thus be rewarded the spoils favored by my boldness.

As I stand with Maria gazing upon the great city, I'm convinced that it's all meant to be.

My phone vibrates.

"Hello?"

"Where you been hiding?" Kenny's hillbilly twang comes through the receiver. "I've got plants down here that could use some watering."

"Been busy. I'll be down there Friday. Need a whole truck's worth."

I hang up the phone.

"Who was that?" Maria asks.

"The guy who made all of this possible."

Indeed, this transition won't be cheap. Until the hotel is fully operational and Maria safely relocated with me in New York, I will continue to fly the merchandise East.

I walk Maria to the end of the boardwalk, where her bodyguard is waiting to take her to JFK. We'd agreed to meet in Cartagena at the end of the month and then drive to Taganga to help Sal prepare the hotel for launch. Then, once it was open for business, we'd fly back to New York and finalize the marriage.

"Be safe," I say, helping her into the back seat of the bulletproof Cadillac Escalade. "I'll see you in a few weeks."

"Promise?" she says.

"I promise."

I lean in and kiss her goodbye.

"Ok, *mi amor* . And try to stay out of trouble."

High speed

I tried, baby — honest, I tried. Can't go with me on this ride, though. Don't feel too bad, I was never supposed to make it this far no how. Really, I'd be lying if I said I was thinking about you at all, busy as I am trying to drive straight in reverse.

The getaway car is an old catering van I bought off a junkie for $500, and while aesthetically a hunk of shit, the acceleration is insane — has the same engine they use in the cop cars, those things chasing me now.

I've got her floored, speeding toward the stop light at busy Martin Luther King Jr. Boulevard. Five unmarked SUVs are coming at me, and the chop of the bird is getting louder.

High speeds are always a tricky proposition — especially hungover. Gotta dump the car and fast — that's your only prayer, big fella. Lose 'em around three corners, then make it a foot race. Spent my whole life running from cops in these very streets, and they ain't caught up to me yet. I know every nook and cranny, alley and shortcut — plus, no fewer than a dozen allies ready to hide me at a moment's notice. Just need to get indoors so I can plot my next move. Fuck, fuck, fuck, fuck — you couldn't have had just one drink and gone home? Had to buy bottles for the whole table, did ya? God, why did you let me fuck squeezer Betty? Maria will have my hide alright.

Almost at the light now, sirens roaring, propeller so close I think it might saw the van in two. Lord, if you wouldn't mind making that light turn — there it is — green. I hit the accelerator and turn hard to the right, swinging the tail of the van into the intersection. I toss her into drive and step on the gas. The van sputters and shoots forward, flying north up MLK. I look in the rearview, and see the first unmarked make a screeching left turn at the light, spinning out of control and slamming into a parked car. In my hungover delirium, I begin to laugh an awful laugh. I'm screaming like a banshee out the window now as tears roll down my face.

CJ's house is less than a mile away, I'll dump the car there and hide in his basement. I've got a bag full of cash that'll get me on a private jet to Mexico, and from there, Cartagena. By the end of the day tomorrow I'll be with Maria in Taganga, dancing on the veranda of my palace overlooking the Caribbean. It's all so perfect. They'd tried to stop me and —

I'm spinning now. Perhaps it's the hangover — nope, I feel a sharp pain in my neck as my head jolts forward. Now the van is resting safely on the sidewalk against a crooked telephone pole. In the rearview, I see two coppers inching forward with their cannons drawn.

"Throw the keys out the window!"

Kissing pavement now, one copper rests his knee in the back of my injured neck while the other one fastens me up. Bracelets always hurt, but this cunt wraps the steel extra tight. Relax, boys. It's only business.

By now, the rest of the squad has caught up, and they're ticked off pretty decent.

"You little cocksucker," one of them snarls and then slugs me in my gut, folding me to the ground like an accordion. "You made me fuck up my car. Why you running?"

"Just felt like running," I wheeze.

"Alright, on your feet," another one says. Through blurred vision, I try and make out the shield hanging from the chain around his neck. Looks like Vice, not DEA — a good sign so far.

Traffic is backed up down MLK as cars creep slowly past the wreckage. Out of nowhere I hear, "Mitchell!"

I look over. A nutty kid called Sias, a buddy from the old neighborhood, is cruising by.

"You alright, dawg?"

"All good!" I shout.

"Keep it moving!" yells the copper.

"Fuck you, cop!" he yells back, blowing on the horn as he speeds off.

More honking and shouting.

"Fuck the police!"

A bunch of Godless commie fucks they are in Portland. I couldn't be prouder.

"Take him downtown. We'll talk to him there," the copper in charge says.

In the back of the cruiser now, I close my eyes – exhausted. You fucked up, big fella. Kingpins don't run, they bail out and fight it in court. It's Friday afternoon. Seems like they always come for you on a Friday, like they want to be sure you spend your weekend in the can while you wait to see the judge Monday morning. Need to focus, but I've got a splitting headache and my mind is doing somersaults.

There's no product in my apartment or at the stash house — all the bricks from the last shipment moved out a few days ago. It was my biggest to date – forty pounds of newly harvested crop from Kenny and Walt's farm. But now, the cops have my duffel bag with $100,000 cash, plus they're sure to find the other hundred or so sitting in the safe next to my bed. Fuck, the keys to one of my safe deposit boxes is in there too — say goodbye to another hundred. I've got my brother holding my last hundred — my get-the-fuck-out-of-Dodge money — in a bank across the river in Washington. It'll be safe there for the moment. My lawyer has a $50,000 retainer fee for occasions like these, which he can put towards my bail on Monday.

I need to get word to Sal. I've got his number saved in every one of my burner phones that the coppers will be pouring through at this very moment.

Sal! My eyes jerk open in terror. No. It can't be him. He texted me last night to confirm the arrival of the merchandise. No way the Vice could've procured a warrant and organized a cross-country raid in just a few hours — they would've had to have been sitting on me for a few days now, at the very least. Besides, if Sal were the rat, it would've been the DEA at my doorstep, not these local swine.

So, how did they find me? I just moved into the apartment a few months ago and I have nothing in my name. Nobody even knew where I lived, just CJ and a few neighborhood skanks, and — I'm sitting up straight now, my body soaked in sweat — my courier! He called in sick this morning! He must've gotten popped with the work driving back from Kenny and Walt's farm on Monday. I'm nauseas now. If it's him then I'm finished alright. Could be his old lady, too, that motherless ingrate sow. Should've seen this coming. They were always bitching about how I didn't pay enough, threatening to strike out on their own, those rotten feckless nothings. You'd be living in your parents' basement if it wasn't for me!

I rest my head despondently against the bars of the window. They'd caught me slippin' alright — snoozing on the job, thinking shit was sweet. Should've known something was wrong when I started feeling good of late, like everything was right with the world. Paranoia is a pusher's best friend — his default setting, his canary in the coal mine perched on high alert for the first signs of danger. It's when he allows himself to finally relax — to give paranoia the night off — that the countdown to his inevitable demise begins.

And I'd been so close — just a few months shy of getting out completely. No matter, this is just a little speed bump. I still have my property in Colombia, I still have Maria, I'm still winning. After all, you're nobody in this business unless somebody wants you dead.

Interview

Got me hemmed up alright, chained to this desk like Hannibal Lector while they breathe hot breath down my neck like a bull mauling a matador. I'm in court — but not the court you're thinking of – with judges and lawyers and bailiffs, but a court nonetheless, and standing trial is my soul.

You're never prepared for it, no matter how many times you rehearse the defiant silence you see portrayed in movies by the crook smiling in the detective's face — all that flies out the window when confronted by the specter of the next decade of your life confined to a cell. To the seasoned felon, one who's spent time in the system and has no trouble returning to it, a grilling by a team of narcotics agents is a mere trifle — even a bore. But for the novice criminal still deluded by hopes for his future, it is the most frightening of interviews.

"You're done," the head copper states flatly. "I've already got enough cash to make a conspiracy case stick. I don't even need the dope. Not to mention that Mario Andretti stunt you pulled — eluding, resisting arrest, assault on an officer, maybe even attempted murder, why not?"

"You fucked up," the young copper leans in — the one who wrecked his car in the festivities earlier. "Just got off the phone with the DA, a mean old cunt. She's got a hard on for you, boy. Wait 'till you see the charges. It's gonna look like War & Peace."

"No way you've read War & Peace," I shoot back.

This makes them laugh. Maybe I've got them all wrong, these coppers. Maybe they can be reasoned with. Now that we're old friends, let me toss some chum in the water and see if I get a bite.

"You have kids?" I ask.

The older one nods proudly. "Two."

"My first will be here next month," the younger one says, packing a fresh dip into his lower lip.

"That's terrific," I say. "Really great."

I pause, glancing up at the electronic eye in the corner of the room staring down at us.

"What if I told you that I can make a generous contribution to their college fund?"

The older one leans in.

"What was that?"

"You heard me. Gimme one hour and I'll make it happen. Nobody will know but us three."

Throwing out the Hail Mary early. I'm not sure what the going rate for a bribe is, but certainly I've got enough left to pay it — especially to these dime store civil servants with crooked haircuts and second-hand sneakers. Ball's in your court now, fellas. Are you boy scouts, or do you feel like dancing?

The two look at each other, and for a split second I can see they're considering it. They know they've netted a whale, they're just not sure how big.

"Well, whaddaya think?"

The older one points up to the camera and smiles.

"I think we can add bribery to that list."

Sackless hogs! You spineless, neutered nerds! Nobody wants to have any fun anymore! Always white boys that wanna play Jack Ryan, goddamn puritan pricks. If these men were Italian, they'd already be in Mexico on their new fishing boats.

I'm sweating terror sweats and my throat is purged of saliva. You've done it now, big fella. You can't pay off the cops once they've got you in custody, stupid. In my apartment with the door closed, surrounded by a quarter million dollars in cash, would've been the time for palm greasing. But you chose to run.

"There's still a way out of this," the younger one says.

But I don't need to hear the rest to know how it goes. They want me to get up on that stool and sing — sing a loud song about Kenny and Walt in Southern Oregon and all of the many pounds of green gold they're sitting on, waiting to be dispersed. They want me to vomit it up alright — Sal and the Jersey connection, the ones responsible for turning my little racket into an operation big enough for the Man to even bother with in the first place. Like none of it meant anything. No, it isn't enough for these coppers to fell my empire in a single afternoon, taking all that I've worked for. They want me to betray the ones I love. They want me to grovel, they want me to beg, they want me to confess that up is down and down is up and two and two equal five. This is the trademark of the Beast — its highest, most essential command.

"You know how the game goes," the older copper says softly. "Save your ass while you still can."

And there it is, the mentality sinking the ship of humankind — get yours and yours alone. If turning on your brother is part of the game, then I'd say motherfuckers have this game twisted. In the trial for my soul, let the jury find me not guilty, for that is one crime I did not commit.

"Take me to my cell," I mutter, staring down at the floor.

A few hours later, I'm dressed in county blues making my phone call.

"Mama, it's happened."

"I know," she says softly, too distraught to be mad.

"Listen Mama, I need you to call the fat man and tell him to get the bail money ready. I'll see you on Monday. I love you."

I hang up before she has a chance to say it back, choking down the tears welling up in my throat. "Guard!" I yell to the C.O. in the glass booth. He hits a switch and my cell door slides open.

They've got me in the high security wing of the Multnomah County Jail — 24-hour lockdown in this bitch. That's fine by me, all I want to do is sleep.

I lay down on the steel slat they're calling a bed and stare out the window. Autumn in Portland is of the Gods alright. Below on the street I watch the citizens enjoying the warm evening, coming and going and shopping and talking and holding hands, oblivious to their fellow men trapped in cages just ten stories above. I close my eyes and think about Maria for the first time all day. Sorry babe, I tried — can't go with me on this ride, though.

Then, for the first time in over six years, I fall into a deep, dreamless sleep. A guilty man's sleep.

Part III

THE SYSTEM

2010-2013

The Beast

This game is a motherfucker, no doubt you're beginning to see. And to think — it was all good just a week ago…

Arraignment — the first bite of the Beast on its way to swallowing you whole. It's Monday, and I've just spent a hellish weekend tossing and turning on this steel slat and forcing down jail gruel a farmer wouldn't feed to his hogs. One time I did read about a farmer in Canada who killed a bunch of prostitutes and fed their bodies to his hogs. Not a nice thing for the prostitutes, certainly, but at least his hogs didn't have to eat shepherd's pie from the county jail.

My hands and feet are chained as I'm marched through the bowels of the Multnomah County Courthouse. I remember visiting this place as a kid on a school field trip and marveling at the men in blue jumpsuits being perp-walked down the hall like circus bears. Now, all these years later, it is I who is on display for the elementary school students shuffling through the halls, holding their sack lunches and staring at me inquisitively. As we pass, I hear one of the kids whisper to his teacher, "Do you think he killed someone?"

"Maybe," the teacher replies. "But probably it was something more common, like touching children."

That'll make them behave alright.

When we reach the courtroom, I'm made to enter through a special door at the back reserved for bailiffs and inmates. Standing in the inmate pen now, I'm surrounded by a shield of clear bulletproof glass. A damn shame — I was hoping someone might be good enough to take a few shots at me and put an end to this misery once and for all.

Civilians are entering the courtroom now. I see my parents walk in and take a seat on one of the benches in the front row. Corpses they've become, pallid and wrinkled — it's like they've aged twenty years since Friday. For a split second I grow indignant — how dare you show up to my arraignment looking slovenly! Sure, I too look like walking death, but I'm eating feces and sleeping on concrete. What's your excuse? Mother, would it kill you to throw on some rouge and a layer of lipstick? Father, is it such an inconvenience to run a comb through your hair? Easy, big fella — this is only the beginning of the aggravation. Save that anger for the enemy. She should be arriving any minute now.

From the back of the courtroom, I spot the fat man come bursting through the swinging doors, huffing and puffing as he waddles up the aisle and over to my corner.

"Sorry I'm late, kid," he wheezes through the glass. "Picked the wrong day to take the stairs."

He takes out his handkerchief and dabs the sweat forming in the craters of his bald head. The veins in his gigantic nose are throbbing purple and he's gasping for air like an overheated French Bulldog. This is Gorski, my lawyer. Gorski is a drunk, and a Polack — but I don't hold that against him. He's also enormously fat, which is the reason I retained him in the first place. I figured a lawyer with that much money to eat must be winning a lot of cases.

"Get me out of here, Gorski," I say. "I'm going mad in this place."

"I know, kid, just relax. Let them read off the charges and then the judge will set bail. We can post this afternoon."

"Did you find out who the rat is?"

"I figured it was [censored] like you said, but their name isn't in the discovery paperwork. I'll know more after I talk with the district attorney today."

"Oh yeah, and who's this DA I keep hearing about?"

"I'm not gonna lie to you," he says, sucking deeply on his inhaler. "She's a cunt. One of those fucking crusaders types. She's running for state's attorney this year."

"Great. Let the fucking begin."

Things have gone from bad to worse to dreadful — a prosecutor with political aspirations is an executioner in a business suit. DAs are the dogs that Clinton let off the leash in the '90s with his crime bills and mandatory minimums, stripping power from judges and handing it to the likes of Rudolph Giuliani.

A blonde woman enters the courtroom and proceeds down the aisle.

"There she is," Gorski whispers. "Wendy Halligan. Don't look at her."

No chance of that, fat man. Her long, sinewy legs are wrapped inside black silk stockings. Her shoulder-length golden mane is so lush and bouncy I could get my hand stuck in it, and beneath her tasteful business suit I can make out two fat tits bouncing up and down with her stride. I begin to stiffen in my Bob Parker, county-issued polyester pants. For a second, I forget my predicament and become overwhelmed with embarrassment by my decrepit appearance.

"GOD DAMN," I say aloud as she has a seat at the opposing table.

The broad tasked with flushing me down the toilet is a piece of ass.

"All rise," the bailiff orders.

The judge emerges from his chamber and ascends the high seat. He's a crochety old white muppet, droopy-faced and with the countenance of a man who's passed out many millennia-worth of prison time. He mumbles some legalese into the microphone, practically drooling as he does it.

"The prosecution may proceed," he says to Wendy Halligan.

"Alright, get ready," says Gorski. "She's gonna try and throw the book at us. But don't worry, most of the charges will get dropped outright."

I like that Gorski is placating me with pronouns like "us," as if he were locked up in here with me. He's kissing my ass, and that's what I paid him for.

"Your honor," Wendy begins. "On September 10th at approximately 11:45 AM, officers from the Portland Drugs and Vice division attempted to execute a search warrant at the residence of Mr. John Douglas Mitchell."

She proceeds to drum up the drama, playing out the story like it was the OJ chase. During the retelling, my mother looks over at me — rightly horrified — but all I can do is shrug. I fucked up, Mama. I fucked up good, but this is the boy you raised.

"While his reckless attempts to elude law enforcement endangered the community and the arresting officers, we feel as though his criminal ties as an entrenched drug trafficker supersede the state's need to prosecute."

"What the…" Gorski says – he's on high alert now, the purple veins in his nose are pulsating.

"In light of new evidence, the state is hereby dropping all charges against the defendant and will be turning the case over to the U.S. Attorneys' office, effective immediately."

It takes a second for the horror to catch up. I turn to Gorski, but he can't look me in the face — neither can the judge, nor Wendy Halligan, not even my parents.

"Very well," the old judge raps his gavel. "Case #383572 will be referred to the federal prosecutors' office. Defendant shall remain in custody in the meantime."

Gorski finally looks up at me, nodding his enormous head in conceit.

"It's the Feds, kid."

I've done it now. I feel the bailiff grab my arm and start leading me away, back down the long esophagus towards the dark, empty pit of the Beast.

I look over at the benches and see my mother crying into my father's shoulder. You owe too much to the game, big fella, and now not even those alligator tears can get you out of debt. All I ever wanted was to be free — since the day I first held that sack with fourteen grams in it. Trouble is, seems like this game forces you to give it all back, as though your freedom is a temporary loan rather than an eternal gift.

Oh well — if it's to hell they're sending me, then it's hell I look forward to. Can't be worse than this fucking place.

Tres Letras

Always heard about the three letters — those three infallible letters that signify your time is up. Never dreamt we'd meet face to face, though. To me they'd always been extra-worldly, mythological, an Illuminati of sorts, operating in the ivory tower of my imagination rather than as flesh and blood humans with car payments and mortgages.

How strange then, that I should find myself sharing a room with two of them now. Must mean that I've made it.

They look like local pigs for the most part, except their badges are shinier, their boots are more expensive, and their bald heads are shaved extra close. When they speak, the stain of cock on their breath is even more pungent.

No sooner had I arrived back at my cell from arraignment, I got the call — Mitchell, you have visitors. Now, I'm seated in another anonymous room on another anonymous floor in the maze of anonymous rooms and floors stacked like hamster cages inside this evil, impregnable castle. I look up at the ceiling — no cameras in this room.

"I want my lawyer," I say — not that fat Gorski can do much for me now.

"Call him later," the tall bald head says. "We wanna talk to you first. I'm Special Agent Alvord, DEA. And this is Special Agent Ruiz," he beckons to the brown bald head standing next to him. "He's assigned to our Latin America division."

"Just got back from Colombia," Ruiz says, grinning. "You've been there before, haven't you?"

Oh my, and how the dominoes continue to topple. Can I at least get a kiss before the screwing starts? Satan has stolen my tongue — now all I can do is nod.

"That's what I thought."

He has a seat at the table across from me and opens a manila envelope.

"Now, tell me everything you know about this man," he says, placing a photograph in front of me.

Lounging poolside — flanked by a haram of Colombian models in string bikinis — is Andres, flashing his patented Colgate smile like a man who has the world at his feet.

That should've been me — happily ever after. I gave my life to this game. I loved and cherished her, honored and respected her in sickness and in health. I stayed true and never crossed her — stuck to the script like the OGs said — and in return, she tore my heart from my chest and stomped it into ground beef. This game must be a cold piece, boy, if this is her way of showing she doesn't love me back.

"Never seen him before," I say, but I feel the fight leaving me.

"No?" Ruiz snorts. "How about now?"

He tosses another photo onto the table. This one makes me turn pale.

He's so mangled I almost don't recognize him, lying face up on the sidewalk with blood oozing from gunshot wounds to his head and chest. His mouth is agape and his eyes frozen wide with dread in the final moments before his expiration. It was the only time I'd seen him not smiling.

"Somebody hit him while he was leaving his office in Cartagena last Wednesday. Killed the bodyguard too."

"I didn't do it!" I sputter.

It's the only thing I'm fairly certain of at this point. My hands are trembling, and my blue county jail jumpsuit is wet with sweat.

"We know you didn't," Ruiz snaps. "A nice white boy like you wouldn't bust a grape in a fruit fight."

"But we think we know who did," Alvord says. "When's the last time you spoke to Maria Fernanda Gonzalez?"

The room is spinning now, and the neon light from overhead is fading to black. I suddenly recall the conversation we had on the Jersey boardwalk last month — when she'd convinced me to marry her.

"Don't worry about Andres," she'd said.

She was going to kill him all along, and marrying me was her ticket out of the country. Andres had never been planning a move into cocaine distribution — that was just the story she used to get me to go along with her.

"We know you've been in contact with her," Alvord says. "Colombian authorities already pulled her number off a cell tower and matched it with texts she sent to your phone last Thursday."

Indeed, the night before the world ended. I'd been at the club getting properly annihilated off booze when she texted. I told her I was in bed and that I'd see her tomorrow in Cartagena. The last thing I ever said to the love of my life was a lie. Turns out, she'd been lying too.

"All this over some weed," I mumble absentmindedly.

"You think I flew all the way up here from Colombia over a couple pounds of pot?" Ruiz says. "You're even dumber than I thought."

"Andres Gaviria wasn't just an international money launderer," Alvord says. "He was a DEA informant."

"My informant," Ruiz says, growing hot.

"No fucking way!" I blurt out.

How much harder was the dick of life planning to slap me across the ass today?

"Yes way," says Ruiz. "He's been on our payroll for a decade. How else do you think a guy that high profile never gets caught?"

He makes a point, and I've read enough history books to know as much. The *Tres Letras* have been employing criminals since the beginning of the Cold War — ones far worse than Andres.

"We need a recording of Maria admitting to the murders," Alvord explains. "We'll get you out of jail right away so you can call her and arrange to meet in Colombia. Do that, and you walk for the forty pounds of grass."

She deserves it alright, the lying, murdering, back stabbing tramp. Plus, I'll do anything to spring from this place — my sanity is fast disappearing like the last grains of sand through an hourglass. I've still got a hundred thousand in cash that the coppers didn't find, and if our hotel in Taganga hasn't already been seized, I'll meet Sal down there and we can start anew. There's still time — I can still win. And helping put away a murderer, well, that might finally set my karma straight, even if the man she killed had been her rapist.

"Make up your mind, Mitchell," Ruiz snaps. "If you don't hop on this deal, then your boy sure will."

"My —"

Ahhhh, but of course. I sorta figured it was him from the beginning, but my brain wouldn't allow me to acknowledge what my heart already knew to be true.

Oh, Sally baby. I was your brother, and you were supposed to be my keeper. I suppose it's all my fault, really. I've always known you to be a selfish prick, and especially now that the Fish has a hold on you the way it does. I knew if you ever got jammed up it wouldn't take much twisting to get you to cry "uncle." A shame alright — we could've conquered the world together.

"You need to pick smarter business partners," Ruiz chuckles. "The state troopers busted him and a couple of dudes unloading a mobile storage unit full of weed in broad daylight. Sounds like he coughed you up pretty quick. We were gonna let the local fuzz deal with you here until we made the connection with Maria and Gaviria. But that's your bad luck, I guess."

"So, what's it's gonna be?" Alvord says, pushing a third photograph across the table.

I look down. It's a mugshot of Maria from years ago, when she was still a street urchin lifting wallets off of tourists in the wealthy *barrios* of Cartagena. Instantly, the love I felt for her comes surging back, and I miss her so bad I have to physically clutch my sides to ameliorate the agony.

"Will you help us convict her?"

"I've never seen this woman in my life," I say, looking the pigs in the eye now.

This madness has gone on long enough.

"Why you protecting her, Mitch?" Ruiz is losing his patience now. "She don't care about you, dawg. She was using you for a green card — you were just the first sucker to come along and take the bait. All this over some lazy-eyed pussy."

"Watch it," I mutter.

The rage simmering in my chest refills me with life.

"Besides," he says, setting his coffee cup down and leaning over the table into my face. "You don't help us with this, and that makes you a co-

conspirator in the murder of a federal informant. We're not just gonna take you down. It'll be your pal CJ, your brother, your parents — anyone who ever accepted a dollar from you, we're gonna—"

I send the Dunkin Donut's cup flying, splattering dark roast all over the front of Ruiz's shirt. Oh, boy. You ought not've done that, big fella.

There passes a moment of silent shock between the three of us — the longest of our lives. Then, Ruiz sweeps the palm of his calloused hand clean across my face, sending me sprawling backward. My head collides with the cement floor, and now, finally, I can get some sleep.

Bitch Slap

Boy, I haven't been bitch slapped like that since, well, Colombia.

I'll never forget that slap, though I can hardly remember it all, trapped as I was in the drunken clutches of third world debauchery.

I'd only just arrived a few days prior to the capital city of Bogota, where I was treating myself to some R&R before continuing the journey north to meet Sal in Cartagena. I was lodging at an inn situated in a rather nefarious sector of town, albeit charming. Hillside cobblestone streets were lined with corrugated tin-roof shops and restaurants. At night, it became a cesspool of scum — drunkards, thieves, beggars, and whores — ambling about like injured wolves in search of easy prey. I was the drunkard in this open sewer, patronizing the local gin joints until the wee hours, before I'd be tossed out and made to find my way home amidst the pitch-black alleys and winding narrow streets that comprise *La Candelaria* .

One rainy evening, near blind from booze and cartel candy, I stumbled into the foyer of the inn, where I happened upon the most dazzling Colombian *mulatto* these weary eyes had yet seen. She was a handsome lass alright — jet black hair that trailed down to her buttocks, full red lips, glowing olive skin, black lustful eyes, and a set of perfectly natural fake breasts — the way the good Lord intended. Instantly, my mind turned to carnal cravings — I'd move heaven and earth to feel my stud inside of her for one minute. The only problem was the man she was with.

He was a pale faced *gringo* , a boorish oaf, with thick glasses and an unkept lumberjack beard. If he'd been wearing overalls and chucking bales of hay with John Steinbeck during the Great Depression, it would have been more fitting than carrying on this pathetic fauxromance with a hutch so out of his league. His massive, glob-like frame swayed back and forth drunkenly, and he struggled to keep his eyes open as he tossed back another swig of tequila from the bottle.

I saw my chance to step in. Colombian women are a proud race, so it was imperative that I open with a real zinger — a romantic wisecrack to show her what a *galán* I could be.

I pulled a wad of pesos from my pocket.

"How much for the fuck?" I ask. "Will forty thousand do it?"

Boy, this really got her going. She started stomping around and waving her hand wildly in my face, shouting obscenities and being all sorts of rude.

"Yo no soy puta!" she kept repeating. *"No soy puta!* You think I'm gonna fuck you for a lousy five dollars?"

She had a point — this did seem low. I'd done a poor job of converting pesos into dollars, but I've never been any good at math.

"How about twenty?"

My second offer went over about as well as the first. She kept insisting she was no whore, which was ridiculous, of course. Nobody this caliber of beauty would receive a root from such a monstrous abomination of DNA like this ugly bastard standing before me — not without significant remuneration, anyway.

She was standing firm, insisting that he was in fact her boyfriend. Since the carrot didn't seem to be working, I tried a more direct approach. I began insulting him in Spanish, calling him everything under the sun — a real wax poetic if you will. I told her she was going around with a lame, a cuckold, a faggot, a retard, a hayseed, a dingbat, a blockhead, a pathetic zilch, incapable of bedding down women in his own country so he'd set sail for foreign shores, hoping to trick a commoner such as herself into receiving his stalk in exchange for a warm room and a few pieces of silver.

He just stood there, the dimwitted ape, chugging tequila and fighting to keep from tipping over, oblivious to the damnations I was hurling at his fox. But then suddenly, the giant awoke from his slumber. Like a boxer getting pummeled on the ropes, this ogre had been biding his time, waiting for an opportunity to deliver the knockout punch. Quicker than a coiled snake attacks a field mouse, the ogre landed a flawless, open palm slap square across my face.

All noise in the foyer came to a sudden and violent halt. Employees and patrons checking in for the evening stopped what they were doing to look at us. They were expecting a showdown. This is Colombia, after all — nothing less than a duel to the death could satisfy this transgression.

My cheek was stinging something fierce, even more than my pride, which was cushioned by my utter and profound inebriation. I gripped my empty beer bottle, preparing to smash it over the man's oversized head. He stared me down, and I stared right back, like two gunslingers in the Old West.

He belched loudly, easing the tension.

"Show some respect," he slurred laboriously, his bloodshot eyes rolling into the back of his head.

And at this, I stood down — for the man was quite right. I had underestimated his ability to speak Spanish. More importantly, whore or no whore, I had insulted him in front of his wench — and for that, he had demanded and received satisfaction.

I decided to extend an olive branch. He was my countryman, after all. Surely there was a way for both of us to win. I opened my wad of bills and flipped through them until I found a U.S. hundred.

"My friend," I said, holding out the bill. "Will a hundred do it?"

"Mitchell!" someone yells.

I turn around, but there's no one there. I turn back to the ogre and his whore, but they've vanished, too.

"Mitchell!"

There's a great pounding, and then suddenly a bright light appears before my eyes, wresting me back into consciousness.

"Mitchell, wake up," the C.O. is wrapping on the cell door. "You got a visitor — some fat guy."

How long have I been in solitary? Two months, I think. Or is it three? I'm stretched out on the cement floor like a cadaver, but I prefer it to the steel cot, which my legs dangle over painfully. I've constructed a mattress made from thousands of sheets of toilet paper, and while I won't call it comfortable, I am sleeping soundly enough to dream — the worst kind of torture a man can put himself through in here. A man's dreams manifest when he still has hope, and in the box, there isn't a more useless emotion than hope.

Entering the visiting room now, Gorski is there waiting for me. I'm so happy to see the fat man I could cry. He's gotten impossibly fatter since we last spoke, and I think I smell Taco Bell clinging to his sport jacket.

"How ya holding up, champ?" he says, as I have a seat at the table across from him.

I notice a fleck of sour cream clinging to his chin, confirming my suspicions. I'm so hungry I have the urge to lick it off.

"You ready for some good news?" he asks me. "The Feds are gonna toss the conspiracy case."

"Don't tease me, Gorski. I'm in no mood."

"I mean it. They can't find the deed to the hotel in Taganga, and with Gaviria dead and Maria missing, there's nobody left to tie you in."

"What about Sal?"

"Sounds like he's stopped cooperating, cause now the U.S. attorney wants to make a deal. They want this whole mess with Gaviria to go away quietly."

So, the fat man was finally earning his meal. For the first time since getting locked up, I smile. Can't be unlucky all the time, big fella.

"What am I looking at?"

"Forty-eight months for the pot — maybe less if I can work something out. The longer you can hang on in here, the more pressure we can put on the prosecution to adjudicate."

I close my eyes and take a deep breath.

"How much longer?"

"Six months, maybe more."

Breath gone now, it feels like the fat man himself is sitting on my chest, crushing my breast plate.

"How am I supposed to survive in this place for another six months? Do you know they feed me shepherd's pie three times a day?"

"You don't have a choice," Gorski says. "Welcome to the system. Hurry up and wait — especially with the Feds."

"Listen to me, Gorski. I don't want to hear that shit. If you don't bust me outta here soon, I'm liable to go batty!"

"What the hell do you want me to do? They denied you bail. I'm not the one who told you to run from the cops and splash a cup of coffee on a DEA agent."

Boy, if he's not right. Time to go all in.

"Gorski, tell them if I have to spend one more night in the hole, I'm gonna kill myself."

I'm bluffing, of course. I only wish I had the courage to die of my own hands, but I'm a coward alright.

"Honestly, that would be easier for everyone," he mutters under his breath, "but don't do it. They're transferring you to Inverness this weekend. It's not ideal, but it beats being in this place."

Splendid. I'm so filled with gratitude to be leaving this torture chamber I want to fall to the floor and kiss the fat man's shoes. Hard to imagine my life could devolve into such wretchedness that news of my impending incarceration is actually a marked improvement. But that's how it is in the system. There is no good — only totally awful or just ordinary bad. They've taken everything material from me. Now all that's left are the years of my life.

I stand up and turn around, letting the C.O. cuff me and lead me away.

"I'll visit you soon, kid," Gorski calls out. "Keep your head up. Things could be a lot worse."

"Get me a good deal, Gorski," I say. "And next time, bring Taco Bell."

Goodbye

Dear Papa,

Word has reached me of your deteriorating health, and so I write to you now, knowing it shall be our final correspondence before you are delivered from this mortal coil. I pray you are reunited with your love, Betty — my Nana. She has been gone five harvests now, but not a day goes by that I do not reflect fondly on memories of she and you and I and those summers spent on the prairies of Okotoks, when time stood still.

'Twas a lifetime ago, Papa, that you taught me how to shoot a rifle and swing a golf club — or during the winter, to hit a slapshot. I cherished the simple pleasures with you, like watching the Flames play hockey on television, and when they lost — especially to an American team — you would lose your marbles and start cursing NHL commissioner Gary Bettman for ruining the league. And you would call him a Jew, and then me and my brother would laugh and laugh even though we didn't know what a Jew was.

I fear the good times are over, Papa, and the laugher we shared so abundantly has been replaced by tears. A great sadness has settled over the land, like that dreadful Albertan winter, which always seemed to arrive too soon.

As I write to you now, I sit trapped in a human zoo, awaiting adjudication for alleged high crimes against the state. They're calling me a trafficker — a purveyor of sin. They claim I profited shamelessly from the weakness of man and his penchant for vice, and perhaps they are right. But can this same avarice not apply to so many "legal" enterprises? What of the pornographers peddling smut across the inter-web, corrupting an entire generation of young men? Or the gambling barons lording over Las Vegas and Atlantic City — entire economies engineered to bleed a man of his last nickel. And let us not speak of the pharmaceuticals! A trillion-dollar racket of death disguised as benevolent, life-saving science, hooking the young and the old as firmly and completely as a needle of Afghani H. Indeed, my humble little trade seems innocuous compared to the havoc wreaked on society by these unscrupulous pastimes. Yet it is not they, but I, who shall be remanded to the gallows.

I've been here nearly two months now, in a jail called "Inverness," where the condemned are kept as they await the fall of the gavel. None have been found guilty — though most surely are — either too poor, too dangerous, or in my case, too much of a flight risk, to free themselves on bond. A melting pot of society's rejects they are, Papa, stewing in a broth of anger and dejection. Day and night, they keep this placed enveloped in chaos.

Gangs of various stripes and ethnicities control each wing of the jail. Even the queers, the homos — draped in pink uniforms which delineate them from the God-fearing prisoners — even they have managed to carve out a slice of the sordid jail economy.

Heroin and methamphetamine are routinely smuggled in through men's orifices, in a method known as keistering — as in, "I shoved this up my keister." I even happened upon a bunkmate of mine, a young colored fellow, smoking a marijuana cigarette in the bathroom. When I asked him how he was able to procure such a fag, especially in an environment where each man is made to strip naked and expose himself to the sadistic jail guards, he simply laughed at my naivety. "I shoved it up my ass," was his reply, before sucking the final embers of the fag down his throat. Although I, too, enjoy the occasional toke after Sunday mass, I can't imagine smoking a reefer coated in my own shit — but addiction is a baffling disease alright.

At night, we're frequently roused from sleep by the guards, who storm the wing with the gusto of SS officers at Kristallnacht. All of us inmates are made to line up against the wall — grown men standing side by side in our pink county-issued underwear — watching as the guards toss our bunks in search of drugs and weapons. This is not entirely without precedent, as the county jail is teeming with both. The preferred weapon of choice is called a shank, which can be any fine tipped object — usually a pencil or a whittled-down toothbrush — used for sticking a man. The other is the ox, which is a razor or a box cutter used for slashing. Because the ox is too bulky to fit inside a man's anus and must therefore be brought in by a crooked guard, this weapon is more common in jails and prisons on the East Coast, where corruption runs even deeper than it does here. Still, anything can happen — and did, last week, when an inmate in an adjoining wing gave a buck-fifty razor slash across the face of a rival gang member. The man is expected to survive, although that's about all that's expected of him. To call this "living" would be a gross abuse of the word.

Aside from the occasional flare up of violence, the days move along with hideous regularity. Each moment that passes is another grain of sand lost to the hourglass of my life, never to be replenished. The longer I languish in this hell, the more my body, mind, and soul wither away, like a flower without sunlight. Hurry up and wait is the law in here. Hurry up and wait for the wheels of the justice system that never seem to turn. I shouldn't complain, though — it's common to meet men who've been fighting their cases inside the belly for years. Imagine that horror, Papa. We're like a petrified bowel movement trapped in the lower intestine, waiting on the courts to give the final push that shits us out to freedom — or more likely, into the toilet bowl of the penitentiary.

I usually pass the days reading, or watching television, or playing dominoes with a few friendly men from my bunk. But mostly, I think about the future. What does life hold for me if I make it out of here alive? Where shall I go and what shall I do? Most importantly, WHO shall I be? My former business — besides the money and all of its attendant privileges — provided for me a sense of identity. Now, who am I? At the moment, I am "Mitchell" or "Scumbag" or "Shithead," depending on the mood of the guards who run the wing. I am even less than that — I am inmate number 577890, a statistic. Sometimes late at night, when everyone has finally gone to sleep, I'll lay in my bunk and think about Maria, and Sal, and CJ, and then I'll drift away on the sweet memories of years gone by. I was free, Papa. So free I didn't know what to do with it all.

I am in a constant state of discomfort, usually from hunger. The slop they serve us is not only horrendous, but meager. Budget cuts, we're told. Always with the budget cuts. Money to lock us up, but no money to feed us. Now, my ribs are exposed and I'm pale and cold and my face is sunken like one of Angela's Ashes.

To make matters worse, I've got the clap. I'm a bit ashamed to admit it, but the night prior to my arrest I'd laid with a floozy from the neighborhood who'd everyone had had a turn with. I'd been mixing spirits and cheap port and had neglected to shield myself. Now I'm stuck in county with the clap, and all they'll give me for it is aspirin. I'll eventually pee it out, they say, but there's no telling how long that'll take and I'm worried I'll have permanent damage to my nether regions. Day and night my rod aches, and when I pee it burns and drips like an old man's nose. I spend most of my time in the bathroom now, shaking off the drops that never seem to stop dripping, like a busted pipe in a Section 8 building.

Currently, I'm being housed in a high-security dormitory of the jail, where I'm surrounded on all sides by men preparing to vanish from the face of the earth. Proper crooks they are — smugglers, thieves, rapists, and killers. Most are facing numbers so astronomical that it's almost cartoonish. My fate is a drop in the bucket compared to them, and as such, I keep it close to the vest. I've learned to never ask another man of his impending sentence, lest my soul dissolve in an acid of sadness at the punishment that almost never fits the crime. Instead, I try and enjoy the comradery, like how a fellow in battle develops a kinship with the other soldiers in his platoon. Many in here are decent men — especially the career villains, who've accepted their lot with a measure of civility and self-respect.

It's the addicts — the junkies and the crackheads and the tweakers — who make life in here insufferable. They arrive at all hours of the night, shoveled off the street like stray dogs. They all seem to know each other and greet with the familiarity of classmates at a reunion. They're loud, filthy, and crass, but worst of all, they seem to be enjoying themselves! Makes my skin crawl, Papa. Can you imagine? A life so ruined, so finally and thoroughly extinguished of any hope, that to be stripped of freedom and tossed inside a cage is a welcome alternative to life on the outside — a vacation of sorts.

The only time a junkie doesn't enjoy himself in jail is when there's a panic on — a panic, meaning the heroin supply has dried up. This is when the junkie experiences his reckoning, during the withdraw. The worst sound in the world is the earsplitting cry of a junkie withdrawing from heroin. Sleep is impossible during one of these comedowns, with the moaning and the crying and the wailing and the shivering and the begging and the black bile shooting from his mouth. When a junkie can't sleep, neither can anyone else — and woe to the man disturbing the sleep of some two hundred walking dead men.

One night, while a junkie screamed in hysterics from his bunk, someone decided they'd had enough. A group of colored inmates descended on the man. One stifled his screams with a pillow while the others took turns beating him something savage. He must have passed out or been knocked unconscious, for he soon fell silent. Serves him right, the fucking junkie. I know it seems cold, Papa — like I've lost my humanity. But the truth is, it was stripped from me the moment they marched me through those gates.

So here I sit, the man without a chair when the music stopped. My empire — at least the one I'd created in my mind, the way every man creates an internal fiction by which he narrates the days of his life — is gone, and the only remnants are a few fading memories and a dose of the clap. Now all that's left is to await the judgement over my fate, so they can hand me my bus ticket up north. This game is like life, Papa. Doesn't matter how much you win — in the end, it WILL kill you.

I must go soon. They're calling us in for chow, and while I detest the cuisine like a sickness, my belly is crying out for it. Funny how we humans, even after all these years of evolution, are still programmed to fight for survival, forgetting that we're all as good as dead, anyway. At least they're serving us warm apple pie for dessert, so that is something.

Well, my old friend, this is where we depart. I on my journey, and you on yours. I am sad to see you go, and shall pass the rest of my days bearing a hole in my heart for not getting to hug you one last time. As you slip into your final hours, whether that be days or weeks from now, I encourage you to let go of your ego, and to forgive yourself and others for the transgressions of the past. You have much to be proud of when you look back on your life, aside from the material success — the five beautiful children and the litter of grandchildren who are *now having their own children, who still choose to name their offspring after you, Doug Thompson, the one who set the table so the future could eat. Even more important than all of that, you stood up to life, and death (they are one and the same) and said, no — fuck YOU. And that is something.*

Now, close your eyes. You see? There is nothing to fear — there never was. Goodnight, my sweet king. Please give Nana my best.

Your Grandson

Apple Pie

I wake up sweating, chest heaving — had a dream the judge threw away the key again. This isn't my bunk. This isn't my dorm. This isn't my blood stained on my shirt either.

I told him not to fuck with my apple pie.

I was so excited for that apple pie I almost didn't mind the shepherd's pie entrée, making it the fourth night in a row we'd been served this inedible sludge. I forced it down in a flurry — my eyes watering — then the mash potatoes, steamed veggies, a bun with butter, and a cup of sugarless tea.

That out of the way, it was time to go dancing. I lowered my head in prayer.

"This is my pie, there are many slices just like it, but this one is mine. My pie is my best friend, it is my life. Without my pie, I am useless."

The apple pie is the best thing on the jail menu by leaps and bounds — junkies trade drugs for it, fags fuck for it, and gangsters fight over it. Perfectly warm, with the correct disbursement of apple junks, it is chased with a touch of cinnamon and rounded out by a wondrously flakey crust. It is, quite literally, all I have left in this world.

But, no sooner had fork speared pastry, a voice of evil came calling over my shoulder.

"I'm gonna need that apple pie, homie."

I looked up. A giant Native American man called Woozy — aptly named for his eyes that stayed locked in a heroin droop — stood towering over me. Woozy is one tough Injun, face so crowded with tattoo tears I'm not sure he'll have room for mine. He's charged with kidnapping and murder, and since the day he hit the dorm he's been making the rounds, harassing and extorting unchecked.

The chatter in the dayroom fell silent as two hundred sets of eyeballs turned to face us. I cleared my throat, but before I could lodge an objection, Woozy swooped down with his fork and harpooned my apple pie, flinging it onto his tray.

"Pie check, PUNK," he said, and sauntered away to his table, laughing with the other members of his tribe.

A murmur swept through the dayroom as the gossiping inmates turned to look at me, shaking their heads in pity.

"That nigga got punked out," a man said loudly from a black table, and their section erupted into jeering laughter.

The men seated at my table grabbed their trays, and without looking me in the eye, stood up and walked away. I don't blame them — punks are contagious in the joint.

Too stunned to speak, my face burned with shame and I could feel hot tears flooding my exhausted eye sockets. Lord, how much more shall I bare? What kind of merciful God doth taketh his child's apple pie?

Enough of that now, big fella. You knew this was coming sooner or later. Nobody can live on the main line in county jail without first passing the entrance exam.

"Punk" is a dangerous jacket to wear in this place. Let everyone find out you can be bullied, and it'll be ants to a picnic. A slice of apple pie can quickly elevate to a weekly extortion payment, and then eventually an ox across the throat. Acts of punkery like Woozy's had to be dealt with swiftly and harshly — the way the Allies should've stopped Hitler the minute his Panzer tanks rolled into Poland.

I picked up my empty tray and deposited it with the kitchen orderlies before heading back to my bunk. Dinner was ending, and the inmates were fanning out to the movie hall, the rec area, and the small outdoor basketball court tucked away at the back of the dorm. No cameras out there alright.

I reached under my bunk and pulled out a small tub of Vaseline, then I smeared a glob across my cheeks and above my eyebrows — war paint. I grabbed the copy of Don Quixote I'd been reading and tucked it into my elastic waist band, then I laced up my sneakers.

He was playing dominoes at a table with some other Redskins when I approached.

"The court," I said.

"Fists or blades?" he asked, not even bothering to look up. He knew what time it was.

"Fists," I said, then turned and marched across the dayroom toward the basketball court.

Slowly, and without drawing attention to the C.O. on duty, the other inmates began to follow. This was the most exciting part of the week — when the boiling cauldron of tension and animosity finally spills over into a gladiator match.

I stepped through the door onto the square cement court, surrounded on all sides by thick walls rimmed with razor wire. As I awaited my opponent, the onlookers formed a human circle around me, blocking the view from inside the dorm. Over their shoulders, I could see a scuffle breaking out between two men in the dayroom, distracting the C.O. and allowing us enough time to do battle. Just then, Woozy emerged, stepping through the human chain to face me in the circle. I could see the tip of the pen he had hidden in his right hand — evidently, he didn't trust his fists, either. It was time. Lord, make my feet swift and my aim sharp.

It happened so fast I could hardly believe it myself. With both hands, I let Don Quixote slam into the side of his head. His droopy eyes widened in shock and for a split second he opened up, letting the pen slip from his grasp. I seized on it and gave him the hardest right hook I could muster, landing my bony fist squarely onto his fat native snout. Blood went leaking, and the crowd went roaring. He regrouped, grunted, and then charged, stumbling onto my foot with the full force of his weight. I cried out in agony, but this was cut short by his enormous fist connecting with my chin, sending me sprawling to the ground. My face scraped the pavement as I rolled to avoid his foot stomping down on my rib cage, then I bounced up. More whistles and shouts of delight from the crowd.

"Get him!" someone yelled.

I moved in, giving him a two-piece to the head and gut. He retaliated with a haymaker that landed perfectly over my right eye, blinding me and sending a sharp pain ricocheting through my skull. I saw him reaching down for his pen — this red bastard was bent on finishing me off alright.

I raised my leg and kicked my size thirteen shoe as hard as I could into his face. He fell to the ground, more blood leaking from his nose. I jumped on him, wrapping my arm around his thick neck and squeezing with all my mite.

"OHHHHH!" came the shout from the mob.

I swear I'll kill him. No drug ever felt as good as draining the life from your enemy.

"C.O.'s coming!" someone shouted, and the human chain dispersed.

I stumbled to my feet and pulled the bloodied Injun up with me.

"Fucking punk," I stammered into his hear, gasping for breath. I was sweating violently, sucking on air and sobbing like a child after a spanking.

Woozy and I quickly joined the line of inmates spinning laps around the court just as the C.O. came running in.

"The fuck is going on in here?!" he bellowed.

I lowered my face as I passed him, but it was useless. My right eye was completely swollen shut, and I had Woozy's blood coagulating all over the front of my T-shirt.

"Mitchell! Turn around!" he yelled and blew on his whistle. "Nobody move!"

"I fell playing basketball," I said as he slapped the cuffs on me, digging the steel into my swollen, bloodied wrists. I gasped from the pain and finally let the tears fall.

"Easy!" the other inmates shouted. "He was just playing ball! He needs to go to medical!"

The C.O. — a drunkard named Collins, turned me around.

"Who were you fighting?" I could smell the Peppermint Schnapps on his breath. It reminded me of Christmastime and all of the merriment I'd be missing out on.

Over his shoulder, I saw Woozy slipping through the door back into the dayroom. Pressing his shirt against his nose to stop the bleeding, he quietly made his way over to the movie area and had a seat in front of the TV.

"Who were you fighting, Mitchell?" the drunkard Collins repeated. "You got one more chance."

But there ain't shit he can say to me. I'd proven to the animals in the zoo that Johnny Boy Mitchell wasn't no punk — and he damned sure wasn't no lily-lipped stoolie, neither.

"Fell playing basketball," I said.

"Alright," Collins sighed.

He led me off the basketball court and through the dayroom toward the exit door. Through my good eye, I could see Woozy, watching me as I marched triumphantly passed our peers who'd only minutes before had had me pegged for a mark. He nodded, and I nodded back. I'd passed the test.

Still in the same clothes now, still with his blood stained to the front of my shirt, for the first time in months, I am alone. I've missed the solitude so much I barely notice the clap stinging my unit with every piss and my jaw aching with every swallow.

A C.O. wraps on the cell door.

"Mitchell, Captain's giving you thirty days. I'll get you in to see medical after chow."

I mutter something incoherent from my searing jaw, then I roll over and close my eyes.

Sleep might be death's cousin on the outside, but for the living dead locked behind these walls, she is the angel of mercy.

Batter Up

How do people arrive at this clandestine archipelago? Hour by hour planes fly there, ships steer their course there, and trains thunder off to it — so it was under Stalin's Gulag, and so it is here in the people's United States. Week after week, month after month, I witness the business of recycled human flesh churning with the efficiency of a Fortune 500 company.

"The system is broken," the bleeding hearts contend.

Nay, it is working marvelously, only broken inasmuch as it breaks down the men it swallows into fractions, numbers on a spreadsheet to be analyzed at next quarter's budget meeting.

"THE WORLD IS A BUSINESS, MISTER BEALE!"

And business has never been better — not even under Ronnie and his Christian Warriors. Indeed, it was that baby-kissing lizard Bill Clinton who conceived of three strikes and ended parole and work release — for what would happen to the bottom line if the beast started spitting out more men than it swallowed? Why, that would be a violation of the immutable laws of business, and by extension, the Universe.

Cousin to the fast food industry, best friends with the garment industry, and mistress of the telecommunications industry, the beast is inextricably intertwined with these American behemoths.

Just like the beef business, here in county they keep us penned inside 24 hours a day like livestock at a slaughterhouse, sardined on top of one another while we wait to be corralled onto the big bus and shipped off to one of the innumerable islands along the archipelago. And while we wait, we feast on beef even deader than ourselves, sold to the beast by the same purveyors who supply the low-cost poison at fast food chains, hospitals, and high school cafeterias. And while we eat, we're dressed head-to-foot in gear stitched and sold to the beast by garment barons with lifetime contracts, industrialists who fetch double the price for what they would get for their wares on the open market. Then, after dinner, we call our loved ones on pay phones operated by usurious private phone companies who'd make an 18th century French tax collector seem benevolent, charging up to $10 a minute in some states.

And on it goes, from the warden's salary to the C.O.'s pension fund — billions a year, men like myself earn for the beast simply by bobbing around in its stomach.

"Don't get caught next time," Black Roger chuckles, slapping his domino down hard on the table. He ain't never lied.

After a month in the hole for fighting Woozy, I'm back on the main line enjoying my newfound respect. I've got stripes now, and motherfuckers are offering ME their apple pie.

Day and night, the dorm buzzes with gossip, as inmates talk and trade info and offer advice over each other's cases.

"He's done."

"He's got action."

"His/my lawyer is a dump truck."

These are the typical phrases used to describe the status of one's criminal complaint.

To have "action" is to mean that the Man's case against you isn't airtight, and in rare instances, even completely spurious. Maybe one of every few hundred men locked up in county is wholly innocent of his charges. Action means you've got hope of winning, and that you may well choose to take matters all the way to trial — or accept a cushy plea deal from the prosecution before that happens.

To be "done" means just that —*ya estuvo* . Fucked, washed, finished, damned by overwhelming evidence — to plead or be found guilty and sentenced to a nice, long vacation.

Finally, to have a "dump truck" for a lawyer is to mean that you are poor and have been assigned an attorney by the courts — one who is also poor and drowning in dozens and dozens of similar cases. A dump truck will fight for you about as effectively as Grenada fought against Ronald Reagan's invading army. It's another way of saying that you're done. Most of us in here are done.

In my bunk area alone, the five of us collectively face a cool century. There's Chepe, a former lieutenant for the Sinaloa Cartel. He's been down almost two years fighting the Feds for conspiracy to sell two pounds of meth. He's got camel-through-the-eye-of-a-needle odds of beating his case, and he'll hang as surely as the sun will rise and set.

Then there's Osito, an oversized teddy bear from a village in Colima. He was trimming in one of the vast Cartel weed fields peppered throughout the dense Siskiyou Forest, not far from where Kenny and Walt had their operation. He'd been barefoot at the time the Feds raided, but he still managed to escape and make his way back to central Mexico without a dime in his pocket or shoes on his feet. He'd let some years go by before he decided it was safe to come back, but a federal warrant was waiting for him. Now, he's facing a mandatory dime, plus years for the guns they found at the grow site. Oso is destitute and dirty and speaks no English, so he'll be strung up by his feet alright. In the newspaper, I read that legalization could be on the state ballot as early as next year — but I don't tell Oso that.

In the bunk next to mine is an old black criminal called Earl, a sweetheart of a man with salt and pepper hair and a smattering of dark orange freckles on his cheeks. He looks just like Morgan Freeman in *Shawshank Redemption,* and indeed, he'll soon meet the same fate. A career crook, Earl is seventy-six years old and has spent more time locked up than I have on earth. He got his start doing B&Es in the late 1960s, but when he became too old to climb through windows, he switched to doing bank jobs. But because Earl is a kind man and not inclined to violence, he chose to simply pass notes to the teller rather than brandish a gun. Now, he's passed his last note.

Finally, there's Black Roger from Chicago.

"Not black cause of my skin, but my heart. Niggas in the hood used to always say, 'That boy Roger heart don't pump blood — it leaks oil.'"

An ex gangbanger and three-time felon, Roger has spent no less than half of his thirty-seven years behind the wall.

"Crackhead mother, father doing life for murder — you've heard the song," he sighed, slapping down another domino.

But now, he's changed. He moved to Oregon, found a job and a wife and started a family. One night, he let a friend borrow his car to run an errand — but that errand turned out to be a robbery. There was a tussle, and the 211 turned into a 187 — now, Roger is facing football numbers for aiding and abetting. His sheet doesn't help him either, and the D.A. is promising to bury him under the jailhouse if he doesn't take a plea.

"Thirteen years — that's what they offered me, and they can't believe I won't take it. They hate when a black man stands up for himself. They think I should fall to my knees like a good nigger and thank them for showing mercy, but I ain't doing time for something I didn't do. I'm taking these motherfuckers to the batter's box."

Batter up. The first one to the plate is Chepe. He's stone-cold fearless, his demeanor unflappable.

"They don't have any evidence," he reiterates to me in Spanish. "Just a snitch who says I sold him two keys of dope."

I won't be the one who tells him that that's all the evidence they'll need. The Feds are pitching a 98% conviction rate.

Chepe had a solid at-bat. Trial lasted a full week, but in the end, he struck out on pitches. One out.

"He's done," Roger whispered as Chepe entered the dorm on his way back from trial. As he walked over to the bunk, he saw me and threw up his hands.

"What happened in there, mayne?!"

He grinned good naturedly, like a basketball player who fouled out on bad calls. The following week, he returned to court to find out how done he really was. The judge gave him twenty without batting an eyelash. Twenty years for two pounds of meth — imagine if it had been three?

In the dorm that evening, I watched him gather up his belongings. He seemed unmoved by the verdict, his face a mixture of pride and amusement — like he was smirking at the gringos and their silly laws. After he finished packing, he approached my bunk and handed me a pen and paper.

"I heard you're a writer," he said. "I never learned how. I want you to write a letter home to my family. Tell them I love them and I won't be coming home."

Without waiting for my response, he walked outside to the yard and joined his Mexican brothers standing in a circle holding hands, their heads bowed in prayer. He's got a new family now.

Next up to bat is old man Earl. He's charged with robbing eleven banks in seventy-two hours. I'll hand it to him — the old fart can still get around. The evidence against him is flimsy — security camera footage of the side of his face while he was leaving one of the banks — but flimsy seems to have replaced "beyond a reasonable doubt" as the Man's burden of proof.

"A black man's cheek, nephew!" he squawked at me. "That's all they got!"

"They done hung niggas wit' less," Roger said.

"Don't player hate me now, boy. I done taught you everything you know — but I ain't taught you everything I know."

Then we all laughed, the way a nephew laughs at his senile uncle whose jokes he's heard a thousand times before.

The morning of his trial and Uncle Earl was feeling spry — even did a little shadow boxing to get himself pumped.

"Been up against the ropes all my life, youngin'," he said to me as he threw a one-two combo. "But they ain't knock me down yet."

We patted him on the back and wished him luck as he left the dorm, like the heavyweight champ on the way to defend his title. But the champ got knocked out in the first round, guilty on two of the eleven counts. That night, he sat on his bunk looking stunned.

"I don't BELIEVE this shit!" he bellowed, slamming his fist against the wall. "My lawyer was a fucking truck! I might as well have been defending myself!"

Still, he refused to let hope die. He showed me a letter to the judge he'd been drafting over the last several weeks in the event that his verdict went sideways. These letters of personal apology are common in the Beast — a last ditch cry for leniency. I can't fathom begging another mortal for my life as though they've got the power of God, better you strap me to the chair and hit the switch. Regardless, as I read his letter — candid, thoughtful, and articulate — it occurred to me that Earl probably could have found something more productive to do with his life. But he enjoyed stealing, that was his passion, and I'm certainly no moral authority when it comes to wasted potential.

As he headed out the door on the day of his sentencing, I brought him in for a quick hug, to which he reluctantly acquiesced.

"Alright now, 'nuffa that gay shit," he said. "Don't matter how old I get or how long I spend in the joint, I ain't never gonna stop lovin' pussy."

"I hear that," I chuckled, and gave him one last player pound. "Good luck, Uncle Earl."

"Thanks, baby, but won't be needin' no luck. What they gon' do to me? You can't lock an old man like me up — that's elderly abuse!"

He cackled as he ran a pick through his slicked backed conch, then he headed for the exit.

They gave the old man seventeen years — a Mortal Kombat finishing move. A damn shame, but after six decades of ingesting him and spitting him back out, the Beast finally decided it had had enough. The night before he was scheduled to be shipped out to the pen, Earl started coughing and wheezing and had to be carted off to the medical unit. Now, he's breathing through an oxygen tank and walking with an IV pole, trudging slowly toward the dorm exit on his way to catch the bus upstate — probably the last one he'll ever take.

"Stay strong, Earl!" we yelled to him from our bunk.

He managed to turn around and slowly raise his fist — still the champ. He wasn't gone an hour before a new fish arrived to take his place. One goes out, and another comes in. The flesh factory is running like clockwork.

One by one, I watch my comrades go down swinging. The harder you swing, the worse you fall — that's the motto of the beast: "Make us give you your right to a trial, and we'll make sure you never play again."

Oso from Colima saw the writing on the wall and chose not to swing. He pleaded out for the weed plants and the guns, none of which belonged to him, for a dime flat — ten years in the Federales. Won't be seeing him no more.

The pitcher is about to retire the side. It's Roger's turn next. I'm on pins and needles the week of his trial, but he's Kool & The Gang in the crunch.

"God's got my back in this one, John. I can feel it. Plus, my lawyer's paid."

He was right. The trial that was supposed to last a week stretched into two. He was really giving it to those bastards. He'd chosen to forgo a jury trial and present his case straight to the judge.

"Too many honkies in this state for me to get a fair shake," he'd said.

In the middle of Roger's trial, I was paid a surprise visit by fat Gorski.

"Good news, buddy," he said grinning.

He smelled of roast beef and horseradish, and I wished he'd regurgitate it into my mouth like a mother bird feeding her baby.

"They wanna do a deal, just like I thought."

"So, let's hear it."

"The U.S. attorney floated forty-three months, I countered with thirty-five, so we'll probably meet somewhere in the middle."

Strange alright, listening to Gorski negotiate with the Beast over the days of my life like they were haggling over a used car.

"I'm not sure I can hold out much longer," I said.

I've been in county over five months now, and I'm withering to dust. Starving, pallid, and exhausted, I've been shackled and transported back and forth from Inverness to the downtown courthouse over ten times. Hours and hours of waiting and suffering through the mindless yammering of every iteration of junkie and criminal imaginable. Can't wait to get to the penitentiary to chop it up with some proper villains and eat some real food. I hear the portions are bigger and the clothes fit better and I'll get a nice big cell with a TV and be able to lift weights and play basketball and eat ice cream and nap, nap, nap to my heart's content. The countdown to leaving this place is reduced to the nanosecond, each agonizing moment stretched out like I'm tripping on Ketamine.

"We're almost there — just hang tight. It'll be worth it."

"Ok, Gorski," I said, getting up to leave — but then I remembered something.

"Did Maria ever turn up?"

He shook his hippo head.

"Nope, and a good thing she hasn't. Time to let her go, buddy," he whispered gently, patting me on the back.

He's right. Good riddance, though my grudge against her has softened in the time I've been down. She lied to me, yes, but the feelings we'd shared in those incredible months had been God's honest truth. Poor gal — she's probably somewhere in Colombia right now running for her life. I miss her. I miss Sal, too. Wish I could call him and let him know that I'm not mad, tell him I still love him and that nothing can nullify the times we'd spend together in Argentina — when we were young and free and our only use for money had been the next round of Fernet and a thick, round ass from *La Rosa*.

I look up from my bunk and see Roger returning from his final day in court. My heart is in my throat now as I watch him enter the dorm and stroll toward our bunk. Normally, you can tell the outcome of a man's verdict by the look on his face during this stroll — but as usual, Roger's is unreadable.

"What's up, Mitch?" he says. "Let's slap a few."

He reaches under his bunk and grabs the domino set.

We're at the table now, silently arranging the ivory dominos. A few minutes go by without either of us speaking, and then he clears his throat.

"Man, I thought for sure I had those motherfuckers," he grins, shaking his head. "Oh well."

And so, it was game over — he lost in extra innings. I'm so numbed to the pain of bad news that I only suffer a momentary jolt of grief this time, before resetting to a disconsolate apathy that has become my base operating emotion.

"I'm so sorry, pal," I offer, but he dismisses my sympathies with a wave of his hand.

"You're a good guy, John Mitchell. Have you thought about what you're gonna do when you get out?"

I pause. Not a second has passed since the day the Man first appeared at my door that I have not pontificated over the kind of life I could coddle together from this wreckage. A million different ways I'd thought about how I could return to the Trap, only this time I'd have all the kinks worked out. I'd do it safer and smarter and with a better strategy to leverage my dirty dollars as a catapult into the legitimate business world. I could still live out my fantasy of outlaw-turned business mogul — I could still set the table for the future. Until now, I'd thought that.

But as I stared into Roger's dark brown eyes, shattered from a life wasted inside the Beast, I knew then that it was all over. I'd had my shot — my perfect, uncontested layup — that rare moment in a man's life when the winds of history are at his back, when fortune chooses him as the object of her desires. There is no replicating what I and other men of the Trap achieved in such a short period of time. Especially for a hapless dolt like myself, there is no getting lucky twice.

"I have no idea, Roger. I just know I can never do this again."

"Well, the good news is you'll never need to," he grins and slaps down a domino. "This ain't the end of your story, Mitch. The world is better off with you on the outside. Just keep searching 'till you find what you're looking for. Never stop searching."

The dorm lights flickered off, signaling bedtime. Roger stretched his arms wide and let out a satisfied yawn.

"Well, my brother," he said, shaking my hand. "Been a pleasure bidding with you. Remember, before the dawn can come, there is darkness."

That night, they found Roger hanging from a ceiling vent in the bathroom, his bedsheets tied around his neck. By the time I woke up and realized what was going on, they'd already cut him down and covered his body with a sheet. They said he shit himself, that his face was bloated and his tongue hanging out of his mouth like Luca Brazzi.

As the medics wheeled his body out of the dorm, I heard someone say, "I called dibs on the nigga's ramen," and the place burst out laughing.

I smiled, too, in spite of the horror — for it was funny. Life is one sick joke alright.

A week later and I'm back meeting with Gorski — this time, he's got the number.

"Thirty-eight months, including time served," he says. "That's a goddamn good deal."

"I don't give a shit if it's thirty-eight years, Gorski."

Indeed, if I have to wait in county jail any longer, I might take after Black Roger and get off early at the exit.

Dirk

I'm like a vampire, the way I've grown accustomed to life without sunlight. It hits me square in the eyes, stinging them like salt water in an open wound. It crawls over the rest of my face and tickles my skin, how I imagine heroin feels the first time it swims through your bloodstream. I'd forgotten what this warmth feels like — same thing with the sound of music or the sensation of someone besides myself grabbing my prick. I'm like a baby out of the womb as I step foot onto the yard. No more county blues — I'm dressed head to toe in denim now. Time to bid with the big boys.

It really is something, the prison yard. You can watch every movie and reality show, but I recommend paying it a visit to see for yourself. A grassy rectangle field, perhaps two hundred yards in length, is surrounded by a track of red clay. A basketball court and a horseshoe pit are nestled at opposite ends of this field, and pull-up bars dot the yard every few hundred feet — patronized according to ethnic gang. No weights in here — the Man pulled those from the federal system years ago. I guess they were worried that if motherfuckers got any bigger, they'd run through the walls like the Hulk and escape.

It's a gorgeous spring day, and all sets are accounted for. There's the Eses, deeper than the lost city of Atlantis. *Cliquas* of every stripe in here —*Norteños, Sureños, Paisas* — but in the Feds, nobody's bigger than *La Eme* — the Mexican Mafia. As I walk slowly around the track, I pass a handful of them standing on the grass in military formation. At the helm is a drill sergeant barking orders in Spanish. They pause and look at me curiously — this pale, stork-like man, lost at sea. Another shout, and with the discipline of Navy SEALs, the men drop to the grass and begin doing burpees, yelling in unison as they propel themselves from the push-up to standing position —*los soldados*.

Continuing my stroll, I look up at the guard tower looming over the yard like an air traffic control booth. A C.O. in aviator shades leans lazily against the railing, scanning the yard like a lifeguard at a crowded pool. A long-range rifle rests at his side. In times of peace he can relax — even enjoy himself a bit — but when the beef is on, his rifle stays at the ready. One warning shot is all they give you in here, then you better kiss dirt or the next one might have you carried out in a bag.

I pass a group of blacks on the pull-up bar. It's been said they've weakened over the years, their numbers usurped by the whites and Mexicans spilling into the Feds by the boatload as the crack epidemic gives way to meth — but they sure look strong to me. BGFs – the Black Gorilla Family, Bloods and Crips of varying sects — Rolling '60s, Pirus — when things got too hot in LA, they'd fled north on I-5 until they reached Portland. Now, three decades later and their spawn are stretched out in here with me.

A few of them turn and stare as I walk by. Staring is a privilege in the joint. Takes juice, for looking directly into a man's eyes is an act of aggression — a challenge as primitive as wild animals on the Serengeti.

"Do you want some of this mess?" the stare seems to ask.

Not at all, fella.

"How the fuck did HE end up in here?" one of them asks aloud.

I'm still trying to figure that out myself.

After the judge let the hammer fall, I was shipped from the county jail to Coffee Creek, a holding facility where all new arrivals in the state go to be sorted and processed while they wait for the Beast to assign them a home. Strict as a Nazi daycare, it was 24-hour lockdown, plus trips to the hole for anyone caught farting out of turn. My second day there, and I managed to get in a fight with this mean Samoan cat with a greasy ponytail. He cut me in line during chow, then he turned around and punked me to my face in front of the entire cell block — I had no choice but to set if off.

I spent the next five-and-a-half weeks in solitary — rung in the New Year lying curled up in the dark, guts churning with hunger and dick aching with clap. The depravation was staggering, even by normal jail standards. The food rations were halved from the inmates on the main line, and all I was given to occupy myself were four sheets of loose leaf and one tiny pencil meant for midget hands. Jerking off was the only exercise I got — save for the half-hour a day I was permitted to putter around the tiny yard reserved for inmates in segregation. Stress ate away at my mind and body. My face was dotted with painful acne, and patches of hair went missing from my legs and beard.

Finally, at long last, I was assigned an island on the Gulag — the Umatilla Correctional Facility, a maximum-security prison located in the desolate Umatilla Valley some four hours east of Portland. A proper shithole alright.

Two trips to the hole for fighting during my county stretch, and now they're classifying me as a high-risk offender, tossing me into the lion's den. I need to put together at least nine months of good time before I can be eligible to transfer out to a minimum security, but as I spin the yard now, watching the hyenas watching me, I kiss any hope I had of good time or early release goodbye. I think of my late friend Black Roger and what he'd told me in county a few nights before he pulled the plug on himself.

"Forget about good behavior, Mitch. Being good will get you killed. In the joint, it's day for day."

I pass a group of whites lounging by the horseshoe pit. Deep as ever, they might take this prison shit more serious than anyone. In the Feds it's the Nazi Lowriders and the AB — Aryan Brotherhood. A burly man with a bald head and a goatee sees me and raises himself to his full height. He grins and pulls up the front of his tank top, flashing me the swastika he's got tattooed on his midsection.

How should one react when someone in the modern world flashes them their swastika tattoo? Some things you just can't learn in school. I'm certainly not going to salute him, but I don't want to be rude either, so I settle on a respectful nod and quicken my pace.

"Hey!" he yells, but I don't turn around.

"Let him go," someone tells him. "He's got good paperwork."

So, they'd already seen my file — incredible.

Paperwork. All you hear about in the can is paperwork. Either you have "good paperwork"—that is to say, you've committed virtually any crime not related to touching or fucking kids and you aren't a snitch — or you have "bad paperwork," meaning you've committed one or both of the aforementioned. In the irony of this upside-down world, I've met some very bad men with good paperwork.

Relieved when I finally reach the basketball court, I stop to watch a group of black guys playing a ferocious game of 3 on 3. Even in here, they're very good.

A man goes up for a rebound in the paint and comes down hard on another man's foot.

"Shit!" he yells, rolling on the ground in pain, grabbing his ankle.

He manages to stand up and hobble off the court.

"We need one more." his teammate says — looking around for takers.

He spots me idling by. Even slouching, I stand well over six-foot-five. I know what's coming.

"Yo, Slim! You hoop?!" his gravelly New York accent booms off the prison walls.

I just stand there, dumb as ever. I'd been in isolation so long I'd forgotten how to speak.

"Man, come on. I ain't got all day," he says impatiently and passes me the ball. "You're running with us."

And that's that — the tall man's burden.

I take my cue from the others and remove my shirt. I look awful alright — gaunt and pale after months of hunger and darkness. The game begins. I haven't had real exercise in almost a year, and immediately I'm panting and sweating profusely.

Prison basketball is similar to free world ball, except that the burden of proof for calling a foul is much higher. It had better draw blood or cause injury, or the foul will simply be ignored. This in mind, I think it best to hang outside and try to get open for a jump shot. The game is to twenty-one, scoring by ones and twos, with the three-point shots worth two.

I come from behind a screen and receive a pass from the top of the key. I step behind the three-point line and let one fly — swish. Next possession, we run the same play but from the opposite corner. I get open off the screen — another swish. Two more three-pointers to follow from the top of the key. A murmur is growing from the onlookers. With every shot I hit, the cheering gets louder as more and more inmates from different sets gather around the court.

I finally miss long, but manage to grab the rebound, take a few dribbles back from beyond the arc and — wet. We're up seventeen-zero now, four more points to win the game. A small miracle is happening. I'm no religious man, but it feels like God has taken over — as though he knows my butthole is at stake. I barely feel the rock leaving my palm as it arcs beautifully toward the net. Swish. Game point. I'm getting double teamed now, but there's nothing they can do. I dump the ball down low to our big man, who gets swarmed, leaving me wide open in the corner. He passes back to me. I take one dribble, then set the round leather pill on its course. It bounces around and drops in — game time, motherfuckers. The crowd doesn't cheer, more like doubles over, guffawing in consternation at the New Fish and his dumb luck.

From somewhere in the crowd of cackling black men, a voice yells out, "DIRK! That nigga plays like Dirk!"— as in Dirk Nowitzki of the Dallas Mavericks, the hall-of-fame big man with the laser jump shot.

And so, it went. For the duration of my tenure in the Federal Bureau of Prisons, I was known only as Dirk.

The loudspeaker calling us in for chow now, I grab my shirt and begin heading across the yard.

"Good game, Dirk," the familiar voice stops me in my tracks.

I spin around. Standing there, flashing me his pearly-white teeth juxtaposed against coffee-brown skin — the same towering force of nature as I remembered him by — is Sweet Tea. I'm so happy to see him I nearly jump into his arms.

"Motherfucking Sweet Tea!" I yell, embracing the man who gave me my start in the Trap nearly a decade ago.

"What's shaking, Daddy O?" he grins, his baritone pimp twang as smooth as the day I met him.

"Fucking locked up," I say. "What the hell got you in here?"

"Drama with a bitch, what else?" he chuckles.

He's cut off his perm, and his beard is dotted with flecks of grey. On his head, he's donning an African kufi.

"What's with the new look?" I ask.

"Come on, let's go eat," he says, putting an arm around my shoulder. "A lot of shit has happened since we saw each other last."

"You can say that again."

Shabazz

"GOD DAMN, you really took the ball and ran it all the way to the end zone, didn't ya?" Sweet Tea says proudly.

He turns to one of his guys seated next to him at the table.

"Can you believe it? I sold this nigga his first pack, WAAY back in the day, and then he grew up to be a kingpin. Only in America!"

Finishing up lunch in the chow hall now, I'd told him about everything — Sal and the Jersey connection, Andres and Maria and the hotel in Taganga, then Sal's betrayal, and about taking the Vice on a high-speed chase and the DEA and Maria's disappearance and the untimely but convenient demise of Andres — and then finally, about county jail and the fights and the hole and my friend Black Roger, may he rest in peace. It came pouring out of me like water through the sieve of a backed-up dam.

Seems remarkable now, as I listen to myself recount the saga of a generation, that my journey and all the drama that unfolded had begun with Sweet Tea in his living room — flanked by two naked whores — weighing out fourteen grams before my wide eyes all those many years before.

"You should write a book," one of the men mumbles between mouthfuls.

"Yeah, right," I chuckle.

Every idiot in the joint has plans for penning his life story — even those who can't read or write.

An old Latino man with loose dentures walks up to the table. He's got on a cook's outfit and a hair net, and he's carrying a large plastic bag filled with dark red liquid.

"Ahh, right on time," Sweet Tea says, as the man fills up his cup. "Wine Wednesdays, Dirk. Make sure you get a cup."

"*Mi especialidad,*" the old man says. "*De la cocina.*"

I glance over at the guard booth in the corner of the chow hall. The C.O. on duty yawns and spits tobacco juice into an empty water bottle.

"Don't worry about him, Dirk," Sweet Tea says. "That's Jensen. We got him in our pocket."

The old cook fills up my cup with pruno and waits for me to take a sip. I taste it with my tongue — ghastly indeed. The first sip and I'm holding down my lunch, my eyes water and I'm wincing like a sick child being forced to drink his cough medicine. The second swig almost turns me blind. The third and I'm completely numb — the desired state when drinking prison hooch. I hold my nose and toss back the rest of the intolerably sweet concoction.

The cook is still standing there, looking at me expectantly.

"*Qué tal entonces?*"

I cough a little, and because I can no longer form words, I simply nod and point to the empty cup.

"*Órale!*" the cook says happily, refilling my cup.

"Go easy on it, boy," Sweet Tea warns. "Drink too much of that shit too fast, next thing you know you're sucking a dick."

The table bursts out laughing — me included.

"I thought Muzzies weren't allowed to touch booze," I say to Sweet Tea when I've regained my voice, pointing at the red, black, and green Kufi on his head.

"That's Nation of Islam shit," he says. "Those cats don't have any fun. Can't no man tell me Allah is looking down on a nigga for having a few — especially in this place."

Sweet Tea is three years into a nine year stretch for pimping and pandering — what the Man now calls "human trafficking." He'd taken a few of his bottom bitches across state lines for Super Bowl weekend in Vegas — a pimp's busiest time of year. All was going well until the final evening, when one of his hoes caught a trick who turned out to be an undercover agent.

"The bitch turned around and handed me over to the Feds," he shook his head regretfully. "But you know what, Dirk? What I look like as a righteous black man, pimping out one of our sisters anyway? I tell ya boy — I had it coming. Allah is the greatest teacher, and these four walls have been my school."

Since being down, he's clicked up with the Five Percenters, a group of Muslims who are more gangster than religious. Like many a prison-convert before him, he's cut off his perm and stopped frying his hair, kicking off the "yoke of European colonialist beauty standards." He doesn't go by Sweet Tea anymore, either — prefers his new Muslim name "Shabazz." He's found a good trade cutting hair and plans to open his own shop once he hits the bricks.

"Listen to me now, Dirk," he says, growing serious. "You're the first white man to ever sit at this table, and *Inshallah,* the last. As long as I'm around, you can walk the yard and no black man will harm you. But I can't say the same for the other races."

Through blurry eyes, my head drifts drunkenly to an adjacent table. I spot the white rhino — the man who'd flashed me the swastika on the yard earlier — seated at the table surrounded by his bald army, whispering and looking over at me. Our eyes meet — his burn with anger, mine droop in drunken fear. I quickly look away.

"You got a piece?" a light-skinned man sitting next to me asks.

I shake my head. All of a sudden, I don't feel so hot. I'm bent over by this hooch alright.

Without drawing attention, the man reaches down and retrieves something from his boot.

"Here," he says, passing me the object under the table.

I take a quick glance. It's a shank, more sophisticated than anything I'd seen in the county jail —a razor-sharp steel rod the length of a pencil, fastened at the base with a duct tape handle.

"That's for when the war pops off," he says. "I don't leave my cell without it."

"This ain't Club Fed," Shabazz warns. "Motherfuckers get killed in here. Keep your eyes open and your mouth shut, and when the beef is on, choose a mark and start sticking."

Gonna shit my pants alright. I stash the shank in my boot and drain the rest of the pruno. Now it's an emergency. I've got a splitting headache, and I feel the liquid sprinting the wrong way up my esophagus.

"Gotta go," I stammer, stumbling to my feet.

"Hooch got him," Shabazz chuckles. "I told you to slow down!"

I waddle quickly back to the cell block, clenching my butt cheeks tight. Never been so grateful for that cage as I stumble inside, thrust myself onto the iron commode and evacuate with ferocity. I lean over to the sink next to the toilet and begin vomiting up mashed potatoes stained with purple hooch. Streams of shit and puke are exiting my body now like I'm a human fountain. Inmates returning from chow are passing by my cell, laughing hysterically one after the other.

"New Fish caught a bad one!"

Finally drained of liquid, I'm ghost-white and drenched in sweat. I strip naked, pour a bottle of water over my head, then jump under the covers. My teeth are chattering and my head feels like it's being stabbed with a thousand tiny pins. Wake me up when this is over, Lord. Or better yet, maybe don't.

Jimmy

I open my eyes, and the first thing I see are the eagle's wings, soaring proudly between the width of his brawny shoulders. The ink has faded over the years, but the symbolism remains the same — this is a rare bird.

Hunched over the sink shaving his massive head, he appears in his early 50s but he's chiseled like a man twenty years younger — so many tattoos his back looks like a treasure map.

"You left a turd in the toilet," he mutters. "I cleaned up your puke, too."

"Sorry about that," I say, sitting up now. My head feels like I've been bare-knuckle boxing.

"Carlos makes a strong batch of hooch, doesn't he?"

He towels off his head, not a sliver of hair remains on his body, save for the white goatee circling his mouth. He turns around to face me now. He's a tired man, his face beset by an exceptional melancholy reserved only for those who've spent decades inside the Beast.

"You must be Dirk, the kingpin. I'm Jimmy."

"Nice to meet you, Jimmy. I'm sorry again about the mess—"

He holds up his hand to silence me.

"You broke the most important rule of the house — that's to keep this place clean. Keep your feet dry and your bunk neat, and make sure I don't smell your shit."

"Understood."

He nods, then reaches under his bunk and pulls out a yoga mat. He rolls the mat onto the cell floor and begins doing sit-ups.

"Dirk the college graduate," he chuckles between reps. "You must've fucked up good to end up in this place."

"Yeah, Jimmy. I fucked up good alright. I fucked up about as much as a person possibly can, at every turn — from getting arrested all the way 'til now. It's the story of my life, actually."

"Well," he winces, breathing heavy. "You're short-timing, so it ain't all bad. Thirty-eight months, was it? Now all you gotta do is survive without losing your good time, or catching another charge, or —" he groans loudly as he completes the final sit-up. "Getting killed."

"Fuck me! How can I avoid those things, Jimmy?! Especially the last one."

"You got yourself a piece — that's a good start."

Jesus, what doesn't he know? I'd forgotten all about the shank I'd stashed underneath my pillow.

"Get yourself a job, too," he went on. "Something that takes you off the cell block for a few hours a day. Do that, and time will fly."

He's doing push-ups now, making the eagle wings flap. He rolls over, dabbing the sweat from his forehead.

"And be careful who you associate with. You made quite a stir sitting with those spooks in the chow hall today."

"But I'm friends with their shot caller, Sweet — Shabazz. We go way back."

"Look, I got nothing against the blacks. I know Shabazz, and I respect him. But it's a whole different world in here, Dirk, and the law says each man stick to his own tribe. It's the way we keep order."

"But what if I were a Muslim, and my skin just happened to be white? What then? Wouldn't I technically be part of their tribe?"

"But you ain't a Muslim — try and join them and see what they say. Or when the beef is on, see if they've got your back when the *Sureños* or *La Eme* wants to turn you into a fillet. That's when you'll find out who your real tribe is."

"What is this beef everyone keeps talking about? Aren't we all just a bunch of assholes doing time?"

"Kid," he sighs gently.

He's sitting cross legged on the mat now, his eyes closed.

"You talk a lot."

"I know. I'm sorry. I just... I can't believe how the world is sometimes, ya know?"

"What can I tell ya? Acceptance is the path to alleviate suffering."

He's breathing steady now, a peaceful grin settling onto his face.

"Hey, Jimmy... what are you doing?"

"I'm meditating, Dirk. Any more questions?"

A long silence passes. It goes against my rule, but I can't contain myself — I need to know.

"Jimmy, what are you in here for?"

"I killed some people," he murmurs, eyes still closed.

"Oh. I'm sorry."

"You're sorry that I killed some people?"

"No, I mean... I'm sorry it went down like that."

"Get some sleep, Dirk."

He's right — nothing good seems to happen when I'm awake. Slowly, I reach under my pillow, grab my piece, then roll over to face the wall. I close my eyes, shank at the ready position.

Sticking

- I'm a tall guy, six-foot-six. Every day a complete stranger will approach me and ask me if I play basketball — that's the only body type where that's still appropriate — you can't do that to anyone else… you can't ask a fat girl if she shot puts, can you? Of course not. You wouldn't ask a midget if he gets shot out of a cannon, would you?

- Racism is dumb, I'm in jail with these white guys who call themselves the "Nazi Low Riders." Low Riders are a Mexican thing! No Nazi has ever ridden a low-rider — can you imagine Hitler rolling through Berlin in a '64 Cadillac, hitting switches?

- I touch my own dick so much I'm beginning to think I'm gay …

- I'm so woke I won't even say the word "chicken" around black people.

- One of my black friends told me I could say the n-word around him… I was like, "Are you wearing a wire?"

- I've had a lot of STDs, chlamydia ("clap it up for that") "chlamydia" has the name "Lydia" in it, which sounds like a girl from Arizona State who gives it to you. I've never had syphilis—that's a really old STD. You can tell it's old because it has the name "Philis" in it.

"Slacking off again, Mitchell? What else is new?"

The one called Eddie interrupts my thoughts. An amiable Mexican American with sleeve tattoos enveloping his forearms, he calls the shots here in the laundry room. Three months into my stretch and I'm sweating like a slave, folding shit-stained dungarees by the thousands.

At Jimmy's advice, I'd gone ahead and looked around for a job. Shabazz put in a word with Eddie in the laundry room, which I was told is a coveted position compared to other hell gigs, like the kitchen or the license plate shop. But by my second shift, I'd had enough.

"Fuck this. I quit," I'd told Eddie.

"Alright, but you'll lose sixty days of good-time," he said.

So, this is how the Beast retains its workforce for $1.25 an hour? Just like Stalin's Gulag, us prisoners in these United States — usually through bamboozling and other forms of deceitful fuckery — we, too, are conscripted to work. Clothes, license plates, call centers, even heavy machinery — the Beast is not a federation of correctional facilities as much as it is an archipelago of plantations, housing modern day slaves with no hope for escape. And a buck twenty-five an hour is generous, too, compared to the state system — or so I'm told.

"I'm on break, Eddie," I say, putting out my cigarette.

Jimmy's got a line on good drum tobacco, so he's been giving me sticks at-cost — or four packets of ramen noodles.

"You writing your boyfriend a love letter or what, *ese* ?" he giggles and snatches the paper from my hand.

"Dude!"

"What is this shit?" he starts reading it aloud.

"I can't explain it, man. They're like… thoughts I guess. Just things that pop into my head. Observations and shit."

"These are pretty funny, *holmes* ," he says. "I like the one about the fat chick."

"Give that back, man."

"Hey, they throw talent shows in here once a month. You should make these into a comedy routine," he says, handing me back my notes.

"Meh, I dunno. What if I stink?"

He shrugs.

"What if you're good? Either way, you'll still be locked up."

He turns and walks away.

"Finish your break and get back to work. We got a lotta sheets to fold," he calls over his shoulder.

I fold up the paper with my thoughts and stash it inside my boot.

The laundry facility at Umatilla Correctional was converted out of an old warehouse located at the rear of the property on the banks of the Colombia River. I stroll past row after row of industrial washers and dryers and scaffolds with pallets stacked to the ceiling with fresh prison clothes. I love the silence in here — the joint is a maddening opera of intolerable noise that begins at sunrise and doesn't end until lights-out. Bars slamming, toilets flushing, loudspeakers blaring, and the myriad animal sounds of two thousand caged beasts — all enough to drive a sane man batty. That's why this is my favorite time of day — the walk from my cigarette break to the folding room, a vacation from the madness provided by the meditative thump-thump-thump of the laundry machines spinning 'round.

The scream is so awful it nearly splits me in two. Heartbeat on hold now, I hear footsteps running off, and then the sound of life leaving a man. Intermittent moaning as I inch toward the giant yellow bin used for discarding dirty laundry. I peer over the lip of the bin. A man I don't recognize is folded up like a shirt, clutching a bleeding hole in his belly. I look closer — what appears to be the tip of a coat hanger is jutting up through his sternum. Vision is a darkened blur now, and I feel my knees buckling. I have to grab the side of the bin to steady myself. The man looks up at me. He's whimpering and moaning something so hideous that for the first time in many years, I despise death more than I do life. He can't speak, but his eyes are pleading with me, begging that I do something so that my stupid face not be the last thing he sees before crossing over to the other side. I don't blame him. Still, I'd say you're done for, fella. Besides, rule number one through infinity in the can is "shut the fuck up and be quiet."

I lower my head in shame and start walking swiftly toward the folding room.

"Ahhhhh!" comes the man's final cry for help.

This guy's really getting on my nerves. You had to get me mixed up in this shit, did ya? And I was having such a pleasant day.

"Just fuck me, already."

I start sprinting toward the guard booth at the end of the hallway.

I find a C.O. named Becker, a motherless redneck slob, kicked back watching television.

"Hey, fucko!" I yell, pounding on the glass. "Help me! Someone's hit!"

He falls out of his chair getting up, then runs out of the booth.

"Jesus, what the fuck, Dirk?"

Now we're both standing over the man, frozen, as though unsure of how to proceed.

"Well?"

I look at Becker, expecting to see rightful panic from a man about to have somebody die on his watch. Instead, he casually shakes his head, spits tobacco juice onto the floor, then picks up his radio.

"Becker to base, we've got a sticking in the laundry room. Send back up. Over."

"Happy now, Dirk?"

He's in my face now, glaring murder, tobacco juice smudging the grey whiskers of his chin.

"Next time, keep walking."

Trouble

Dear CJ,

This game is a motherfucker, ain't it? Funny how I once thought you the fool for choosing to leave it — especially on the eve of us getting rich — but then we both might be writing letters home.

Must be careful what I put in here now, as the Man reads the outgoing mail — though it's not me they've got under a microscope. My celly is a lifer named Jimmy, and though I can't be certain, I suspect he's got some real juice in here.

Jimmy DeLuca is the biggest gangster I ever met, and I've met a few. He did his first stretch when he was twelve years old — stabbed his math teacher in the neck with a pencil after he wrapped his knuckles with a ruler for misbehaving in class. 'Spose that's why teachers don't hit their students anymore. He made his bones doing collections for the Philadelphia Mob in the late '70s and claims to have met all those famous Waps — Sammy the Bull, Gotti, Paulie Castellano, etc. But because he himself is only half-Sicilian and was thus unable to rank up, he soon left the Mob and began working with the Hells Angels. He was into every racket — gun running, extortion, dope dealing — even claims he was the first to start smuggling in pure crystal meth from Mexico. Whenever Breaking Bad comes on the TV he'll throw a fit. "Walter White, my ass," he'll scoff. "I knew the real Walter White. I sold him the recipe, and then he elbowed me out of the business." But this could've been his own paranoia — by the time the '90s came around, Jimmy was fully sucked up on C, snorting and shooting more than he was selling. When he finally got pinched in a DEA sting, his last act of freedom was to kill the informant and his wife — both ex Angels — before they could make it to trial. Now, he's serving double life.

Sometimes I'll break night listening to his stories, which he narrates with the detail of a Stephen King novel. He remembers everything down to the minute — like his life is frozen in time, an artifact in a museum . Hollywood scriptwriters only wish they had the imagination to invent the tales Jimmy recounts to me in passing, as though he were describing a day at the beach. I let him talk as long as he wants — for when a man has no future, all he's got left is the past.

He and I have grown friendly of late, though there's not much choice but to be friends when you're stuck living in a cement box no bigger than a bathroom. Now and then, when I'm hit by the awful reality that Jimmy will die in this place, I become consumed by a sadness so profound that any attempt to describe it here would be an understatement. Instead, I focus on my immediate priorities, the most pressing being my own survival.

Right now, I should be hitting golf balls at some cushy Club Fed resort with white collar crooks and other short-timers — but instead, I'm here at Umatilla guarding my asshole. Oh, and about that, you can rest assured that Johnny Boy has not been turned into a fanook — praise Allah. Prison rape is mostly a hype, anyway, from what I can tell. It happens, surely, but like rape in the real world, it is never a pleasure-seeking act, but a power move. If all one desires is a carnal release, in here it can be procured like a stick of gum. "Six months to the gate" is the golden rule — that is to say, six months prior to one's release, one must desist with his homosexual activities, lest he be rendered a full-time donut pumper. Seems mighty convenient if you ask me. I'm almost at my six-month cut off, so if ever there were a time to use my hall pass and take a man in my mouth, it would be now.

In here, one can stumble upon gay sex like a landmine in Vietnam. One evening, I had the misfortune of happening upon a man taking another man from behind in the shower. Two black fellows, flawlessly muscular and hairless, power topping and bottoming with the strength and synchronicity of a college rowing team. It was like watching two Alaskan grizzly bears grappling over a salmon — both beautiful and terrifying. A few days later, I saw one of these men from the shower in the visiting room surrounded by his wife and kids. I withhold judgement, for I am short-timing, and one day soon — Inshallah — I shall draw a free breath and again feel the joy of a woman's touch. This man might not be as lucky. I try and remember that when I am on the basketball court and the fellow guarding me from behind grabs me a little too low on the waist, sliding his big hands 'round my buttocks. I could make a scene, but then later I might end up as the meat in a black shower-fuck sandwich. Besides, if I can ameliorate one person's suffering even for a brief moment, well, then that is a good thing.

Weighing heavy on my mind lately is the sticking — that is to say, a stabbing. Having a piece jammed into my gall bladder or an ox run across my throat, like a Mexican man on this very cell block a month before I arrived. The other day in the laundry room, I witnessed...

I can't go into detail, but there's trouble afoot. The gangs stay ready for battle like Cherokee warriors, over what I can only presume is control of the drug trade. And it is booming alright. No surprise that the men who've perfected the craft on the outside have evolved to perpetuate it inside these walls. And it ain't chump change, either. One stick of reefer — a tenth of a gram rolled tighter than fish pussy inside a piece of notebook paper — trades for $7 on the yard, so imagine what a toot of meth can fetch? A single balloon containing two or three grams can keep an entire cell block high for a week. You can always tell when a balloon has gotten through — a relieving wave of calm settles over the institution, like morning sunshine after a stormy night. In the five or six days it takes for those shiny crystals to circulate the prison, there is less arguing, less fighting, less killing — all things that could potentially fuck off one's high are moved to the backburner. Perhaps this is the reason the jailers allow it to pass through — well, that and a thousand bucks a month, wired anonymously into a crooked C.O.'s bank account.

Drugs are all that is left. Deprivation drives the ideology of the American Gulag, and year after year, it grows worse. It began when parole got the guillotine in the early '90s, followed by conjugal visits, naked photos, cigarettes, furloughs, education programs, work release, even the weights — anything to remind a man that he is alive and that perhaps he still has value — it has been purged. There is no "correction"— the price is penance. You will pay for what you've done, today and every day for the rest of your pitiful existence.

A buzzer sounds. The cell door slides open and Jimmy enters, unbuttoning his shirt.

"Preparing your will?" he says, hopping up onto his bunk.

"What's that, Jimmy?"

"You're a dead man walking, aren't you?"

"What do you mean?"

"Your buddy, the one who fell on a coat hanger in the laundry room the other day? He's gonna live. They had to remove his lower intestine to get the hanger out, but it missed his arteries, the lucky fuck."

"Thank God," I say, breathing a sigh of relief.

Haven't slept since that day — too scared to spend time with my dreams, as it were.

"Not so lucky for you. He's a snitch, Dirk."

I spin around to face Jimmy now.

"Are you sure?"

If that's true then I'm in deep trouble.

He nods.

"He was trading info to get his sentence reduced, helped put a RICO case on some AB guy's last year."

This keeps getting worse. The Aryan Brotherhood is the least-fucking-around group of psychopaths in the entire Bureau of Prisons.

"They finally had him, and you fucked up the hit," Jimmy says. "Now you've got a target on your back."

I'm trembling and drenched in icy sweat. In the can, anyone assisting a snitch in doing anything other than dying might as well be snitching themselves — indeed, might as well be dead. I want to fall to my knees and ask God why, but I've learned long ago this is a fruitless exercise. This is simply my life, and I will never get it right.

"What do we do, Jimmy?"

"We?"

He grins ironically, flipping through the channels on his tiny TV set at the foot of his bunk. The Feds prohibit inmates from having televisions inside their cells, yet Jimmy not only has one but watches his in full view of the C.O.'s, unmolested.

"We… have a sit down."

Disciples

A man with nothing to lose is a dangerous man alright — an unpredictable man, for he has renounced any hope for a future. He has shed the burden of every artificial social and moral taboo and vanquished the ubiquitous but foolhardy desire for modern material gain. All that he owns is his physical self, and all he's got to look forward to is his next breath. Eventually, these too become optional. Let this man overcome his biological imperative to do whatever is necessary to draw his next breath, and you've got a powerful man indeed — a free man. The freest men I'll ever meet are doing life behind bars. Unconcerned by the imminence of their own death, they wield awesome, Godlike power — for like God himself, they decide who lives and who dies.

The summer sun is beating down on the yard as we approach them now — God's disciples. I look up at the C.O. in the adjoining watch tower. No more idle supervision, the beef that's been simmering of late has him standing at attention, trigger finger curled. That's reassuring — at least now if they decide to stick me on the spot, hopefully that guard will be good enough to fill one or two of them with some lead.

You can spot a lifer by the way he moves. I've learned that from watching Jimmy — never in a hurry, he knows these bars will be here waiting for him. Indeed, I see it in these men. They move with intention — no wasted energy. It's like they're pacing themselves on this slow march towards perdition.

As we enter their atmosphere, I spot the rhino with the swastika tattoo on the bar doing pull-ups, his enormous back and shoulders shredding with each thrust. They descend upon us immediately like unwelcome guests in hostile territory. A shorter man with black hair and thick glasses approaches, shaking Jimmy's hand.

"James, how are you?"

He's got a deep surfer's tan, and his dark almond eyes betray an ethnic background far more muddled than a classic white supremacist would prefer.

"Knuckles, meet my celly Dirk," Jimmy says.

"Dirk — that's a good German ballplayer," he says, shaking my hand. "You're the guy who was moving all that weed, right? And now it's about to be legal, meanwhile you're sitting in here doing time behind it. Ahh, well. That's life, isn't it?"

We're encircled now by lookouts with their backs turned to us, guarding against any outside ambush.

"This is the crew — you'll get to know them in time. This here is Butch," Knuckles says, pointing to the rhino man.

Butch nods at me suspiciously.

"Whaddaya say, Butch?" Jimmy asks.

"All good, Jimmy."

He grunts, then turns and spits in the grass.

"Look… Knuckles," I begin. "I want to apologize for what happened in the laundry the other day. I got locked up behind someone snitching on me, and if I'd known the guy was a rat I woulda never —"

"We understand that," Knuckles says. "But by now you should know that the surest way to get yourself killed in here is by sticking your beak in places it don't belong. That's the very reason that homeboy ended up on a coat hanger in the first place. Dig?"

I nod. A strange kind of shame it is, being admonished for acting according to your humanity. But I'm no victim. My simple-ass knew to keep on walking, but I just couldn't help myself.

"We're not monsters, Dirk, so if someone winds up on the wrong end of a piece, you can bet they deserved it. I don't send my men on Kamikaze missions either, like the Spics do, just to have them end up on death row. I spent months planning that hit."

"He knows that, and he's ready to make it right," says Jimmy.

Knuckles grins wryly.

"You've got a good friend in Jimmy, here. Stay close to him."

I see Jimmy's face, and for the first time since I've known him, I think I spot fear.

Knuckles turns to me.

"That guard Becker in the laundry room — he's turned out to be an asset. He's gonna be bringing in the package next week. I need you to pick it up after your shift and deliver it to Butch on the main line. You can start with that, then we'll talk about working off the rest of your debt."

And just when I think I'm out, they pull me back in. Perhaps this drug dealing shit is my destiny after all. Perhaps it's already been written — my fate as a career criminal.

"Sure, no problem," I say.

"Atta boy," Knuckles says, slapping me playfully on the shoulder. "Nothing you haven't done before. Jimmy can fill you in on the details later. You boys take it easy."

With that, Jimmy and I continue with our walk around the track.

"Jimmy," I finally say. "What did he mean that YOU will fill me in on the details?"

He sighs and shakes his head, hesitating for a moment.

"Dirk, what I'm about to tell you, it should go without saying that if it leaves this conversation, we'll both end up dead."

"Of course, Jimmy."

"Alright, well — that dope you're about to smuggle in for the Brotherhood — it belongs to me."

"What the hell does that mean?"

"An old Angel friend of mine on the outside — he's the one supplying Becker."

"You mean you're the fucking kingpin?!"

"Keep your goddamn voice down," he snaps. "I'm not the kingpin, I just have the connect. The AB are the ones who move it, and they have to kick upstairs to me whenever a package gets through."

Boy, I always knew Jimmy had some juice, but as it turns out, he's got the keys to the whole fucking yard!

"Jimmy, this is perfect! Just tell Knuckles I don't wanna do this. Tell them to go get somebody else."

"I don't have that kind of pull anymore, Dirk," he says somberly. "If you don't do this then I can't protect you. I'm a fossil, and the AB knows it. It's only a matter of time before they give me the shove. And in here, there's only one way that happens."

He makes a cutting motion across his neck.

"The important thing is that you get out of here as quickly as fucking possible. You do this job for them, lay low, and before you know it, you'll be transferred out to a minimum security — never have to look at my dumb face again."

At this moment, I love him like my own father, and it hurts to see him be anything less than indestructible. But alas, I suppose he bleeds like everyone else.

"Okay, Jimmy. Whatever you say."

"In the meantime," he chuckles, spitting a tobacco glob into the grass, "stretch that butthole out. You're gonna need the room."

Stand Up

A masked man's gun to my head, a high-speed chase with the law, a cage fight with a killer Injun, even my looming death at the hands of the devil's rejects — none of it matches the fear I'm feeling now — as I prepare to take the stage.

Strange, isn't it, how nothing that came before this mattered? They say death makes a mockery of one's problems, and, depending on how poorly this goes, that may well be what happens.

The mob is out for blood tonight — the gymnasium is pitch black, and I can smell the hooch being passed around. Mouth is dry, heart is hydroplaning, and it feels like Satan is wringing my guts out like a wet rag. I've had diarrhea that began this morning and is only now corking up, for I have nothing left to evacuate.

Standing at the back of the gym that doubles once a month as a theatre for the performing arts, I witness the executions — a spoken-word poet, a guitar act, a political orator, even a puppeteer. One by one they ascend the stage, only to be gunned down by the firing squad. In a full-blown panic now, I look for a way to wiggle out of this. I consider starting a brawl or feigning a heart attack, though that won't take much feigning. I decide to stay and fight — for ain't no flight in the joint no how. That's the thing about being locked up — you've got no choice but to walk straight into the fire.

I need a plan of attack. I'm noticing a pattern with each performer. The first is fear, like one of Tyson's opponents before a fight. It is a subtle but visible tell — a drop of blood in the ocean — signaling wounded prey to the sharks in the audience. Smelling it now, they attack. Whistling at first, sporadic shouting, and then the oranges start to fly. Growing angry, the performer might lash out at the crowd, until the booing starts and the C.O. on duty makes him stand down to avoid bedlam. Even worse is when he attempts to win the mob back — a battered housewife's desperate plea to her abusive husband, but it only makes them boo louder.

The MC named Clyde walks up to me.

"You're on next. Whaddaya want me to say?"

"My name's Dirk. I'm doing stand-up comedy."

I can't recall ever seeing someone feel so sorry for me. He shakes his head pityingly.

"Alight, you get five minutes."

I watch as an old man with a harmonica finishes up his tune, which the mob mercifully permits without threatening mutiny. Clyde shakes his hand and grabs the microphone.

"Give it up for him guys, come on."

Some polite claps, and then…

"This next guy is gonna be doing stand-up comedy. He don't look funny, but hey — let's give him a shot."

No point in being scared now — I'm walking into certain death, like the first guys off the Allied boats at Normandy. Die with your head up, big fella.

"Make it loud right now, for Dirk!"

Every head in the room turns to watch the stork-man taking the stage.

"Oh, hell naw!" someone shouts, igniting the crowd with unanimous boos.

"Y'all niggas shut the fuck up!" a guttural voice comes thundering from the audience.

A few rows back, I see the silhouette of Sweet Tea Shabazz, sitting with his arms crossed like a sagely African general. When everyone has quieted down, he points at me.

"Go ahead, Dirk."

I toss my notes aside — the ones I'd been scribbling that day in the laundry. Won't be needing these.

"What a bunch of fucking losers we are, huh?"

I wait for the sniper shot of boos to hit me between the eyes, but instead it's a wave of laughter — sparking slowly at first, until it spreads like brush fire to the back of the gym.

"I mean, really — whatever the judge gave you, it wasn't enough."

I glance stage left and see the C.O. on duty, giggling.

"What are you laughing at, C.O.? You CHOSE to come to prison."

Wham, a slug to the gut — the belly laughter ricochets off the ceiling.

"I see the Black Gorilla Family is in the house tonight. Way to shake off the stereotype, DUMMIES. My whole life I've tried to convince white people that you guys aren't monkeys — but if you insist."

"DAAAAAAMN!"

That gets them going alright. The blacks are holding each other, stunned by the balls on this skinny pale prick.

"Mexicans, you're here. No conjugal visits allowed, yet somehow your wives keep getting pregnant… you better ask your cousins."

They're screaming — I've got them on the ropes, jabbing and uppercutting as I wait for that bell to ring.

"The Nazi Low Riders are here — there's just one problem… Nazis drive Volkswagens, STUPID."

Rage is shooting out of me like ejaculating lava, incinerating everything in its path.

"They claim to be proud of their white skin, but I caught them on the yard the other day getting a suntan."

I'm whipping them into such frenzy I'm worried a riot might break out, but it's worth it alright. Now for my closer — the knockout punch.

"A lot of you young kids want to get out of here and become rappers. Well, I've heard some of you rap, and let me say this — if your plan to escape a life of crime and incarceration is by becoming a rapper, well then… we'll see you back here. Your bunk will still be warm."

The laughter mushroom-clouds, howling like I've never heard before. There's something here, this stand-up comedy. I haven't felt such power since the days of the Trap — but unlike the Trap, I can share this with people, and together we can commiserate on the torture of life imprisoned here on planet Earth.

"I was in the shower the other day, and this guy started rapping for me, and I can honestly say… I would have preferred a raping. Goodnight."

As I'm leaving the stage, I shake the stunned MC's hand.

"Uh, make some noise for Dirk everyone," he says.

They're on their feet now, applauding for me like I just granted them a presidential pardon.

I'm exiting the gym when Shabazz walks up and gives me a bear hug.

"What the hell was that?!" he shouts in amazement.

He never knew I had such inclinations toward the stage — and until now, neither did I.

I shrug.

"Just some thoughts I had."

Surgery

You don't know what you're capable of — I promise. In our lifetimes, most of us will never realize our full potential, but many more of us will stoop to lows we never thought possible. Never could I have imagined a significant other's pinky fitting inside my asshole, let alone a balloon stuffed with five grams of heroin. Yet here I am — a balloon inside my balloon-knot.

"Push, goddammit!"

Butch is guarding the cell door while I squat over the iron commode, attempting to give birth. Getting it in was easy — the trouble, it seems, is getting it out.

"I am pushing, you motherfucker. It's stuck."

I'd made a point of not eating that day — lest I get nervous and shit myself before making it back to the cell block. Now, I'm begging my Lord and Savior for a good dump.

My plan was to swallow it, but when I met C.O. Becker in the laundry room and he handed me the golf ball-sized balloon, I'd elected for the other end. With the help of some spit and a few packets of mayonnaise, I managed to wedge the balloon snuggly up my shit-shoot. At the end of my shift, I clocked out and headed for the cell block. I walked casually, trying not to cum.

"Just forget that it's in there," Knuckles had instructed me. Difficult when it's pressing against my prostate, challenging my sexuality.

I passed easily through the metal detector in the hallway that connects the laundry room to the main wing of the prison. Elated, I began my stroll towards freedom when I heard the lieutenant bark.

"Hold it!! Line up for skin searches."

Like an Arab at the airport, I'd been randomly selected — or had I? Was it the Brotherhood setting me up? Retribution for fucking up their hit? I thought my knees might buckle. I'd been strip searched more times than I could count, but now I was one spread-em-and-cough away from an extra three years in federal prison. Slowly, I turned to face the lieutenant, a huge chocolate man with a tattoo on his neck. He was holding open the door to a small room used for examinations.

"Come on, Mitchell."

I could've cried, like a kid caught stealing candy. I was trembling as I walked with my head down towards the LT. when I heard his voice.

"I got 'em, Jackson."

I looked up and saw C.O. Becker standing there.

"You sure?" the lieutenant asked.

"Yeah, it's no problem. You got enough to worry about."

"Fine by me," he said chipperly.

He turned to walk away, and then Becker followed me inside the examination room.

"Alright, Mitchell. You know the drill," he grumbled.

Too stunned to speak, I stripped naked — lifting up my feet and hands and ears. I bent over, spreading my sweaty flaps, then I coughed. A long moment of silence passed, and then from behind me, I heard something — it was Becker, sniffing the air.

"Is that fucking mayo?"

"Yes sir, it is."

"Alright, get dressed and get the fuck outta here," he said.

Now I'm back in Butch's cell, undergoing another rectal probe. I'm off the toilet and clutching the side of his bunk, bent over with my ass in his face.

"I see it!" Butch says. "The son of a bitch was telling the truth."

"Hurry up!" one of his goons whispers in a panic. "Line movement's in five minutes."

"I can't push any harder," I plead.

"Hang on, Dirk. Just hold still," Butch says.

I feel a gloveless finger entering my anal cavity, and I jump.

"WHAT THE—"

Butch slams me hard against the wall, gripping the back of my neck with his Teflon hands.

"Hold. Fucking. Still."

He reaches over to his desk and uncaps two blue ink pens, then he goes in for surgery. The scalpels enter my tunnel now, and I have to bite my tongue to keep from screaming.

"Almost there, almost there…."

The pointed BIC pens are scraping against my rectal walls like nails on a chalkboard. I'm lightheaded and praying for the reaper to end this nonsense already.

"Got it!" he whistles excitedly.

Gripping the end of the balloon with the pens like a pair of chopsticks on a dumpling, he pulls hard. *Plop.* It lands on the floor, the blue balloon now stained brown and red.

A momentary ecstasy washes over me as my innards breathe a sigh of relief. Just then, the cell door slides open.

"Get the hell outta here— quick," Butch says, grabbing the balloon and stuffing it into his shoe.

I pull up my pants and fasten my belt buckle, then I turn left out of Butch's cell and join the other inmates on line movement. Grimacing from the pain leftover from my colonoscopy, I limp toward the yard for some fresh air.

"Yo, Dirk!" I hear someone calling from the dayroom floor below.

I look down. It's my friend Pele, the star basketball player at Umatilla.

"You wanna hoop?"

"Ok."

I manage to smile. It's just another day.

What's Beef?

This game is a motherfucker, surely by now you're convinced. For those left in doubt, I ask — what other misfortune must befall me so that you might hear my cry?

Perhaps it's the beef.

The beef is the mayhem that ensues when the tectonic plates of rage and boredom invariably collide, sparking a full-scale riot between prison sets. I'd heard about this phenomenon non-stop since the day I first arrived in the belly, but I hadn't believed it — chalked it up as another Greek myth invented as a mind trick to pass the time. Then again, one can't believe almost anything that happens inside these walls until he witnesses them for himself.

Things are different when the beef is on. It's palpable — sticks to you like jungle sweat, stifling and cacophonous. The yard, usually a firecracker of shouting and cursing and laughing, is now unnervingly quiet. The lookouts mug extra mean, the men on the pull-up bar hoist themselves toward the sky with added resolve, and the C.O.s pacing the towers above grip their rifles even tighter.

When the beef is on, it's common to see men heading to the showers with a towel and a bar of soap in one hand and their work boots in the other. That way, they'll be equipped with the proper footwear to join in the fight — should it pop off while they're showering.

At night, I'm kept awake by the perennial scratch-scratch-scratch from the neighboring cells, as men whittle down their toothbrushes into weapons of war.

Any bond or cordiality that existed between members of opposing sets disappears when the beef is on. The wagons are circled up according to skin color and clique affiliation. It's too dangerous to befriend an outsider, for at any given moment you may be forced to fight him — possibly to the death.

Beefs are a kind of resetting — a disruption to the status quo, a chance for new power to emerge and dethrone the old. A revolution of sorts. Even those not affiliated with a set can take advantage of the beef to settle their own personal scores.

Unlike a military strike, the beef is not consciously planned or coordinated. It is an unspoken, Molotov cocktail of pain that forms organically over time and is made spicier by ingredients like fury and frustration, then shaken over and over again a thousand times until all that is needed is a spark.

I was on the yard the day the beef started cooking.

It was a sticking alright — executed so subtly the C.O.s didn't even realize someone had been hit until after he was already dead.

I snatch a rebound and kick it back outside to Pele, but he's already heading for the exit. I spin around. The entire yard — a sea of men in white T-shirts and khaki pants — is walking silently toward the cell block. They know exactly what time it is.

"Come on, Dirk," Shabazz whispers over my shoulder. "Keep your head down."

I join the throng of inmates on the track moving quickly toward the safety of the building. In the corner of my eye, I spot him — splayed out on the grass by the horseshoe pit – an unmoving, shirtless lump. Never thought I'd see my first dead body on a prison yard, but then again, seems like a fitting place.

A rifle shot pierces the air, and for a split second the only noise that can be heard is the fluttering of pigeons' wings fleeing the scene. Three hundred men hit the earth, face down with their hands on their heads.

The stormtroopers blitz the yard with their riot gear ready, but they're too late. No rioting here — not yet, anyway. Just organized, calculated murder.

It takes hours for the C.O.s to cuff everyone and march us back to our cells. Suspects are hauled in for questioning, leaving the cameras to do the rest — though it's hardly an open-and-shut case. Ten identical bald men dressed in white T-shirts leaves plenty of room for doubt in a court of law. Won't matter much one way or the other. Surely the killers are God's disciples, and a second life sentence would mean even less than the first.

Jimmy is already back in the cell reading a book by the time I return. I collapse onto my bunk and shut my eyes. If only there were a way to constantly be asleep without actually being dead.

"You alright, Dirk?"

"No, Jimmy. I'm not."

"It's nasty, this beef between the Mexicans."

"Was that guy dead?"

"*La Eme's* not in the business of leaving anyone alive."

"What happens now?"

"Cell time — a lot of it. I'd say at least ninety days. After that is when the real trouble begins. Animals in captivity go crazy when they're finally let out of their cage, ya know?"

"FUCK!" I yell into my pillow like a petulant schoolgirl. "Will this shit never end?"

I'm going mad alright. Goddamn to hell my creator for leaving me alone to rot on this cursed, stinking planet. I begin to doze off, but then suddenly I'm ripped from sleep. Sitting up now, it's just occurred to me — in ninety days, I'll be eligible for my transfer to a minimum-security facility. If we're locked in our cells the whole time, there's no way the Brotherhood or anyone else can get to me! With any luck, I'll be long gone by the time the beef kicks off.

"Jimmy!"

I stand up next to his bunk, but then I catch myself — the last thing a lifer wants to hear is the excitement over his celly's impending resurrection. Of all God's disciples, Jimmy sits at the head of the table — and it is he and he alone who shall decide if I walk out that gate or get wheeled out in a bag.

He looks up from his book.

"Yeah, Dirk?"

"Um, what are we gonna do until then?"

He removes his reading glasses, smiling in that paternalistic way I've grown fond of.

"You know, Dirk, you're gonna be getting outta here soon. Time will go by, and then more time, and eventually you'll have a career and a family and a mortgage — all of those square worries crooks like me don't have. And that's a good thing, but part of you is going to miss being in here. And do you know why? It's the only place on earth where time doesn't exist. The past is the past, and the future is just an idea. All we have is right now, me and you, in this cell. So, why not just be?"

"I wouldn't know how, Jimmy."

"Come on. I'll show you."

Be

I breathe all the way in, holding for a second before releasing fully. It is this space between breaths that Jimmy assures me holds the meaning of life and death.

"We're just a collection of atoms, vibrating back and forth rapidly," he explained. "Our minds are constantly moving, dwelling, and worrying because that's how we evolved to survive. They're just thoughts, and feelings are just feelings — they aren't who you are. Who you are is the vibration, that space between breaths."

A month into lockdown, and Jimmy has me on a strict lesson plan. We started slowly, meditating ten minutes in the morning and ten at night, until now we spend an hour on each end. I want more and more, but Jimmy warns against this, too. He warns against any kind of desire, in fact.

"Desire is what leads to suffering," he explains, then shares a passage from the Bhagavad Gita.

"It is the most basic principle of Buddhist thought. When we want something and we cannot get it, it makes us suffer. Even when we do get what we want, it's almost never enough."

Indeed, I thought back to all the levels of greed the dope game had unleashed in me. First it was simply the desire to get out of working a real job, and on and on until the only thing that could satiate me was a million dollars in cash.

We spoke at length about materialism and the torture of trying to accumulate and hold onto possessions.

"This is the sickness of America and the modern world," Jimmy explained.

As part of my journey toward living in the present, he stressed the need for me to forgive, to let go, and to become unattached to people or things.

"This is the concept of impermanence, Dirk. All mental and physical events come into being, then dissolve."

He's right. Every second of my incarceration had been a cycle of self-torture over the collapse of my business and the loss of my money. Boiling with an irascible anger, I'd blamed Sal's betrayal and Maria's disloyalty and the pigheaded cops and the vindictive D.A. I'd wallowed for weeks in self-pity, cursing heaven and hell and society and myself for fucking up the lottery ticket I'd been handed. I'd made myself dizzy with stress, agonizing over the future and how I would survive without the Trap. But now, it was time to let all of that go.

"Breathe in, now let it out," Jimmy repeats.

The weeks continue to roll by with the speed and predictability of an ocean tide. A curious thing has happened — the clouds of stress fogging my mind have dissipated, leaving my thinking clear and my body energized. The tension in my chest, omnipresent from the moment I entered the Beast, has finally eased, replaced instead by deep, unworried breaths.

"Hold it in for five seconds, then let it all the way out."

But as my date approaches, I grow concerned that I might actually be happier inside these walls. Perhaps Jimmy is right. What kind of freedom can one expect to find in the rat race anyway? In here, a man's basic needs are guaranteed, leaving him time to be still — to be human. Inside these walls, there are no such artificial constructs like goals. There is no pressure, no expectation, and — aside from the gang hierarchy — no ladder to climb. Each desire of modern life known to cause a man suffering does not exist in here, leaving only a life lived moment to moment, as Buddha teaches.

When I bring up my concerns to Jimmy, he just laughs.

"If you can be happy in here, you can be happy on the outside. Just remember to be present, and don't take anything too seriously, because all this shit ends. And hey, if it doesn't work out, I'm sure you'll find a way to come back."

We breathe in fully, then we breathe it out.

The prison is stirring again, the inmates growing restless like schoolchildren about to be let out for summer break. Gang signs dance through the cell bars as if the whole joint were hearing-impaired, and the scratching toothbrushes are keeping me up again at night. Word has come down from a top-ranking shot caller. It's a green light — means bodies are going to drop. Whose body is entirely up to us — just pick a mark and start sticking.

The days move slower, and I feel the tension returning to my chest. I keep my ear cocked anxiously for the sound of the C.O. banging on the cell door, telling me to roll up. Almost ninety days into lockdown, and I'm beginning to lose hope.

"Come back to the breath," Jimmy reminds me. "Whenever you feel your mind wander, just come back to that breath."

I breathe deep, holding it in for a few seconds, feeling the vibrations and what it means to be alive. Then, I let it out.

Keyholder

"This sorta thing has to happen every now and then," Shabazz explains as he folds the last pair of faded underwear and drops it into the pile.

Recently, they'd begun letting men out of their cells for essential work duties. When I returned to the laundry room, I was overjoyed to find that Shabazz had been reassigned there. On the many days when it's just he and I folding mountains of laundry together, it feels like we have the entire prison to ourselves.

"It helps to let the bad blood spill," he continues. "That way, things can cool off for a couple of years until the next one happens. But shit, by that time you'll be mister big shot Hollywood comedian. I'll probably be in the dayroom, watching you on TV." He grins.

"I'm not so sure anymore Shabazz. I really can't see myself making it in show business." I shrug as I dump another satchel of smelly socks into the washing machine.

"Come on," he says, "let's go have a smoke."

We step outside to the patio area, gazing beyond the barbed wire at the splendor of the Columbia Gorge as it sheds its yellow summer skin for autumn red. I haven't had a cigarette in months, and the tobacco ignites a dopamine bomb in my brain. We stand there in silence for a few minutes, drinking in the late afternoon sun.

"You hear anything about your transfer?" he asks.

I nod.

"Yep, they denied it. Looks like I'll be releasing from Umatilla, assuming I don't get… ya know—"

"You'll be alright. The Five Percenters know you're neutral."

"But do the others? I'm celled up with head whitey — that makes me guilty by association."

"I 'spose that's true," he says, a growing look of concern on his face.

"Don't worry about me," I assure him. "Besides, you never know — it could be fun."

"Shit, this cigarette got you high, boy."

"You know, Shabazz, this is going to sound crazy, but I can't remember ever being as happy as I have been these past few months. Maybe I've just been down so long that I forget what real happiness feels like, but I can't explain it — it's like the weight of the world has been lifted off my shoulders. I know shit is fucked up, really fucked up, but… I don't care. I'm still grateful. Grateful for this moment, and this cigarette, and you know… just for being alive."

"My nigga," he smiles proudly. "That ain't crazy at all. It means you're finally starting to grow up. I wish I'd had that wisdom when I was your age."

"Well, you're never too old to live," I say, putting out my cigarette, "or too young to die."

"Listen to me, Dirk," he says seriously, "you're gonna get out of here and you ain't never gonna look back. You're gonna go to Hollywood, you're gonna get on stage and you're gonna use that talent I saw the other night, and you're gonna make something of your life. I promise you, one day this'll all seem like a bad dream."

I have to fight back tears as I reach out to shake his hand.

"Thank you, Shabazz. Thank you for everything."

He brings me in for a hug instead.

"Peace be unto you, my brother."

I hug him tight, for I love this man, and love is all that we have — or so I'm told.

"Been a pleasure bidding with you," I say.

It's late by the time I clock out and return to my cell block. I'm tired alright, arms enflamed from folding and tossing and carrying sacks of laundry all day. The Mexicans who work alongside me have knighted me *perezoso* — lazy, for my obstinate work ethic. But I earned that $11.50 today boy, and I ain't never lied.

I'm walking down the long hall toward the cell block when I hear, "Wait up, Dirk."

I turn around — it's Knuckles, leaving the medical unit. He closes the door and trots over to me.

"Let's take a walk," he says.

"I wanted to let you know, you did good getting that thing back from the laundry room for us. Thank you."

"Don't mention it," I say cautiously.

"Heard you had a close call with the lieutenant. I spoke to Becker about it, he'll be on watch to make sure that doesn't happen next time."

"Next time? I thought we were square?"

"I said we'd discuss it. So, we discussed it, and I figure you got one more run in you before we can call it even."

"Yeah, sure. Whatever you want."

"Good. It'll be the same thing as last time, but on this run, you'll get a cut of the profit. Sound good?"

Sounds fishy alright. There's an angle here, though I can't quite see what it is.

"Yeah okay, sounds good."

We reach the gates of cell block C. A buzzer sounds and a door slides open, letting us through. C-block is its own city — four aisles of cells stacked six stories high, thirty cells per story, all told housing over five hundred inmates. I imagine we could burn this place to a pile of embers if we really wanted to — all we need's a match.

"Becker will get with you when the package arrives," Knuckles says, turning down the tier toward his cell. "Oh, and do me a favor, Dirk? Don't tell Jimmy about this. It'd be better for everyone."

I freeze. Jimmy warned me this moment might come.

"Why's that?"

"Look, I don't wanna freak you out," he says, lowering his voice. "But we think there might be another rat —" He nods at me knowingly, "I have it on good authority that it's Jimmy."

"Do you think it's possible?" I say, doing my best acting.

"I know, it breaks my heart too. But just to be safe, don't mention what we have going on, *comprende?*"

"No — of course not, and thanks for the heads up."

He gives me a pound and then turns and walks away.

"Good to see you Dirk!" he calls over his shoulder.

So, it was finally happening. The Brotherhood must've found their own supplier on the outside and connected them with that crooked pig Becker, who sold out to the highest bidder. Now, they need Jimmy out of the way so they can monopolize the yard.

I climb the staircase toward my tier. But what if they're not lying? What if Jimmy is a rat? If there's one thing I've learned in my torrid career in narco-trafficking, is that which seems impossible is highly probable. If Jimmy is a rat and he thinks I know, I'll never make it out of my cell.

"4-D!" I yell to the guard in the control booth. The door slides open, and I see Jimmy with his back turned, shaving his head in the mirror.

He grunts hello as I climb onto my bunk. A long silence passes — too long for a chatterbox like me, Jimmy knows well enough by now.

"Everything alright?"

"I talked to Knuckles."

"Yeah? What'd he have to say?"

"Says you're through. Says he wants me to keister another balloon for him, but he told me not to tell you about it. Says you're a rat."

Jimmy rinses and towels off his head, then calmly walks over to my bunk.

"And you believe him?"

"No."

He nods his head, satisfied.

"He's ambitious, that Knuckles — always has been. He wants the keys to the yard."

He sighs, running his finger along the small American flag pinned to the wall above his desk.

"But there can only be one keyholder, Dirk. You tell him, whenever he wants to come pick them up from me, all he's gotta do is say where."

"Okay, Jimmy. I'll tell him."

We sit there awhile in silence, for there is nothing much left to say.

"What should we do now, Jimmy?"

He turns to me and grins.

"Just be."

14 Grams

And just imagine, Mama — it all started with fourteen grams. One day soon it'll cost as much as a pound of produce at your local grocery store, and the drug war and the dope game as we know it will be relegated to the museum of history — a small pothole on the highway toward humanity's inevitable perfection. Those fourteen grams gave me power, Mama. Fourteen dime bags clutched tight in my sweaty palms — it was like I'd been asleep at the wheel until the moment God stuck a cup of coffee under my nose, awakening within me the unlimited and awesome power of the Universe.

Fourteen grams to freedom — that was my mindset. Like a slave on the underground railroad with nothing but the North Star to guide the way, so too I thought those dime bags would lead me to the promised land, freeing me from the bondage of modern life. And indeed, for a time, they did. Before my eyes, fourteen grams turned to fourteen pounds turned to fourteen thousand a week, booming at my peak.

But as it turned out, this bondage was an illusion, as was the freedom I sought — both clever mind tricks of greed's design. I mistook freedom for the tangible, the bodily ability to up-and-go, to outrun the long arm of normalcy and the restrictions placed on the ordinary man curtailed by a time clock, bills, and a family. It took for the law to shackle my body, Mama — for me to find that the freedom I'd been seeking was never physical. In my fugitive race to elude the responsibilities of modern life, I was in fact hiding from myself, and in turn, from life itself. Life, in all of its beauty and possibility. Turns out everything I'd been seeking is not out there, but in here. And it's been in here this whole time — I just needed to sit still long enough to find it.

Fourteen grams, Mama — gives me chills just thinking of it now. I loved selling dope, and I was great at it. Like the bootleggers of the 1920s, I and men of my ilk shall go down in history as the last of a generation to seize upon the opportunity gifted to us by the laws of prohibition, and, like Al Capone said, "reach out *for the American Dream and grab it with both hands." Never again shall there exist a moment in time like the one I lived through — a brief and glorious era where thousands of men with a little brain and a lot of ambition managed to carve out a slice of this elusive dream. It was an honor and a privilege to be part of this legacy, and although I let the dream slip through my fingertips, I can now say without a shred of doubt that it has all been worth it.*

My only regret has been hurting you, Mama, but I humbly ask that you find a way to forgive me, just as I have learned to forgive myself.

I'm writing to let you know that I won't be coming home as soon as we had planned, and that I may never be coming home at all. In fact, by the time this letter reaches you there's a chance I'll be dead. If this is the case, please know that I didn't suffer, and that I am not suffering now. Suffering is a symptom of desire, and desire is the disease of modernity — a deadly side effect of human progress that inclines men to compare and covet, lust after and compete, invade and conquer — all the while leaving him hollow inside, thirsting for more. A fool's race it is, Mama, scrambling to fill up a treasure chest without a bottom in it, as though that alone can augment the joy of our lives or ease the terror of our deaths. Show me where this has happened, and I'll show you the camel who fit through the eye of a needle. No, Mama — I shall run no more. I contend that happiness is not something to strive for, but inherent in all of us, attainable by all of us — if only we'd stop running.

I will try my best to make it home to you, Mama, but if I do not, promise me you'll reminisce only on the memories of good times past. And only for so long, for it is far better to bask in the gratitude of being alive and the glory of the present moment — for that is all that truly exists.

Strange, isn't it? How it took me to lose everything to realize I already have everything, and always will. Those fourteen grams taught me that, Mama. Though I remain locked away in this cage, for the first time in my life, I am free.

There's just one more thing I must do...

My eyes flutter open — I must've dozed off. Sitting up on my bunk now, I see Jimmy hunched over at his desk, reading my letter. I feign a cough. He looks over at me, startled.

"Dirk," he says. It's the first time I've seen him embarrassed. "Uh, you left your letter out."

"It's okay," I say softly.

"I know it's fucking okay!" he snaps, throwing his glasses down.

He leaves the letter on the desk and starts pacing the cell. He's aggravated. I can understand why. Scary what's about to happen, even for one of God's disciples.

There's a knock on the bars — it's the orderlies coming by with lunch. An inmate in a kitchen smock passes two food trays through the cell slot.

"Kitchen made that lasagna extra special for you, Jim," the man says, then continues on down the tier.

Jimmy nods, then has a seat at his desk. He removes the plastic lid, letting the steam from the hot lasagna billow out over his face.

"Smells good," he says.

He looks underneath the lid. Two rolled-up napkins are fastened to the plastic with duct tape. He removes them and hands one to me.

"That piece you got under your bunk is no good. Use this."

I unwrap the napkin to unveil it — an inmate's best friend. It must be eight inches long, made from a cook's spoon and meticulously whittled down to a razor-sharp tip, then wrapped with duct tape at the base for grip. This is my shank. There are many like it, but this one is my own.

You see, in the joint, there is no peaceful transfer of power — no handshake or retirement party or quantitative easing. Knuckles wants the keys to the yard, so he'll have to come and take them.

The plan is to hit him after he passes through the turnstiles that demarcate the different cell aisles on block C.

"There's a blind spot there by the janitor's closet," Jimmy instructed. "Grab him by the neck from behind and shove him inside. I'll stick him in his front so there isn't as much blood."

Indeed, it would be far easier to kill Knuckles with some quick razor cuts across the arteries in his neck, but that would risk drenching us in a geyser of his blood. Killing a man with a shank is harder — more personal. It requires precision and tremendous force and, above all, hate. Anyone can pull a hit-and-run with an ox, but it takes a real killer to kill with a shank.

From below, I hear the stomp of C.O.s boots come rumbling down the aisleway. In the corner of my eye, at the far end of the cell block, I can see the door to the yard swing open. The inmates are lining up at their cell doors now, shoes on. It's finally here.

"Yard time, Dirk. Get ready."

Jimmy throws on his jeans and his best pressed collared shirt. I double lace my boots, as though that extra knot is body armor protecting me against enemy shanks. Jimmy cleans the stubble off his head with a razor, splashes water on his face, and runs a comb through the white hairs of his goatee. I tuck my shirt into my jeans, fastening the shank just below the belt line. Then I brush my teeth and comb my matted hair, for it's important that a man appear presentable at his own funeral.

Ready now, we stand side by side at the door, waiting silently for it to open. The rest of the cell block is eerily quiet, a prelude to the conflagration that's to come.

A buzzer sounds, and then a C.O.s voice comes over the loudspeaker.

"Inmates, line up for yard."

One by one, the cell doors begin sliding open and the inmates emerge, turning and walking down the tier in the direction of the yard. Almost our turn now. My hands are trembling, and my breath is coming in short, panicked bursts.

"You alright, Dirk?" Jimmy asks.

"Grab him by the neck and push him inside. I got it," I say, my heart rate steadying now.

Jimmy looks down at his feet and smiles, shaking his head.

"You know, Dirk, I never told you this but… I was there that night in the theater when you did your little comedy routine…"

Just a few more cells to go. In the distance, I can hear shouting erupt in the dayroom.

"You were really funny."

He nods his head in concession, as though he'd been debating over whether or not to admit this. I turn to face him, my eyes misting over in gratitude. It is the highest praise I've ever received.

"I think you'd better go and do that," he says.

Our cell door slides open. He steps out first, then he turns, blocking my exit. He puts one hand on my shoulder.

"It's been a pleasure bidding with you, Johnny Mitchell."

"Jimmy, wait a min—"

But then I'm suffocating, no air to form words. A direct hit from Jimmy's kneecap into my groin sends me sprawling to the cell floor. He turns and heads down the tier, leaving me gasping and writhing on the ground like a hooked bass. The pain from my testicles moves north into my stomach and then finally, up and out of my throat. Now I'm choking up fresh lasagna vomit and crying in agony over my nutsack. The cell door latches shut.

In the distance I hear a man scream, and then the crack of the tear gas cannon coming from the yard. The alarm is shrieking, my nuts are throbbing, and my head feels like it's being crushed by a vice grip. Vision growing blurry now, the shouting and the cursing and the pounding of the stormtroopers' boots and the C.O.s whistles and the gunfire — all of it starts to fade into the background like pleasant elevator music, the soundtrack to a dope boys life.

Then finally — mercifully — black.

Epilogue

Silence. The most beautiful sound in the world is no sound at all. A decade later, and I take for granted almost everything I was deprived of in prison, choosing — perhaps consciously — to forget about the bad dream. But not the silence. Never. Real silence is golden — I could listen to it all day like it was Mozart's Symphony No. 40. In those privileged moments when I find myself immersed in true silence, I'll think back to the madness of the joint and become overwhelmed by gratitude.

Like right now, backstage at The Comedy Store — that iconic comedy club on the Sunset Strip that launched all those cats we know and adore — I'm all alone, bathing in the silence as I wait to go on stage. The only sounds are the sporadic machine gun bursts of laughter filtering in from the audience. Fuck, the guy ahead of me is killing. He's charismatic and famous and beloved, and what do I got? Just these thoughts, spun and woven and chiseled and re-worked over thousands of hours on stage and scribbled onto yellow legal paper. Maybe it's too hard after all. Maybe the dope game was the only thing I was destined to be great at — an exceptional blip in an otherwise mediocre existence. I'd just as soon pack it up and move home, but I made a promise to a friend. Well, not exactly a promise — more like heeded his advice.

Jimmy saved my life that day when he kneed me in the balls so hard I couldn't leave the cell. The beef that ensued was the largest in the history of the Umatilla Correctional Facility, and probably the entire state of Oregon — or so I'm told. In the twenty long minutes the rioting lasted, more than ten people were stabbed, two of them fatally. Another, a mister William "Knuckles" O'Brien, died from blunt force trauma to the head.

After Jimmy left the cell, he'd gone looking for Knuckles, but when he couldn't find him amidst the mayhem on the yard, he ditched the shank he was carrying and returned to the cell block. The Brotherhood was waiting for him. As Jimmy turned the corner by the medical unit, Knuckles emerged from a small broom closet, shank in hand. Legend has it, Jimmy didn't even flinch — just hit him one time in the head so hard it made Knuckles' neck snap back, crumpling him like an empty wrapper as his skull crashed against the ground. But it was a suicide mission alright. After Knuckles went down, Butch and the rest of the disciples pounced, sticking Jimmy over fifty times. In the end, it was his only way out of that place. I owe you one, friend.

The host ducks his head into the greenroom.

"He's got the light, Mitchell. You're on next."

I take my position behind the curtain, listening as the performer finishes up his closing bit. I try and shake out the nerves rocking my guts, but they're more stubborn than usual tonight. Reminds me of the first time I ever tried stand-up, almost ten years ago now, for a different kind of drunken audience. But unlike then, tonight I'm free to run. Could duck out the exit doors right now — no motion sensors or barbed wire or C.O.s with rifles impeding my escape. Do the wise thing for once, Mitchell — find a job and a wife and live out the rest of your days with both feet on the ground.

"Can't you just be normal?" my father's words echo in my ear.

Okay, Pop — I'm finally ready to try.

"Some asshole you are," a familiar voice cuts through the silence.

I spin around — it's Sal, stepping out of the shadows, his ocean-blue eyes dancing in the dark like fourteen-carat diamonds.

"Say it ain't so? The guy who had the nerve to traffic dope across the continental United States, sticking up his middle-fucking-finger at the laws of this great nation? The one who had us laundering money around the world like we were some hot shot *mafioso*? The motherfucker who took a federal case to the head and still kept his mouth shut? THIS guy is afraid of some drunken jerk-offs in a comedy club?"

He steps toward me, a cigarette in hand.

"The joint must've really messed with your head."

He looks good — Guido hair is long and slicked back, and he's wearing a three-piece suit. I forgot until this moment how much I missed him.

"Things are different now," I say. "I'm a civilian. If they don't laugh, that feels worse than a life sentence."

He chuckles.

"I got news for you, pal — you ain't a civilian."

He puts his cigarette out on the dirty carpet.

"You know, you've got this fantasy in your head about getting out of the life and setting the straight world on its ear, but me and you know that cannot happen. You ain't got the stomach for it — the square world. You NEED danger, John. You need the thrill — you're addicted to it. Have been since the moment you traded your first dope sack for that dirty ten-dollar bill. Johnny, what the fuck are you gonna do, except hustle?"

The crowd cheers riotously for the comedian as he exits the stage. I look at Sal. He's grinning that mischievous grin — the one I could never say no to.

"Well," he says, lighting up another cigarette. "Get out there and hustle. And remember, the game ain't changed — only the product has."

He turns and walks away.

"Sal, wait."

He pauses and looks back, staring into my soul with those hypnotizing blue pinballs — the one's I'd fallen in love with all those lifetimes ago in Rosario, when time stood still.

"Why'd you do it?"

He shrugs, unconcerned.

"You're here, ain't you?"

Indeed, I may never have found comedy if it weren't for Sal. From the stage, I hear the host announcing my name.

"I gotta go. I'll talk to you after my —"

But he's gone, vanished into thin air. I look over at the floor where he'd put out his cigarette — that's gone, too. Now, all that's left is to take the mic out of the stand.

I come out of the gate swinging. I need to knock these motherfuckers into submission before they have time to counterpunch. My first joke connects, laughter filling up the room, and my soul — if such a thing exists. Sal's right. I can't live without the thrill. Stand-up comedy is the closest thing I've found to the Trap, in that it too is an outlaw's undertaking — one man standing up to the world and saying, "No, fuck YOU." Like the Trap, in stand-up, a man is only as good as his last move — in this case his jokes — and never more than one misstep away from agonizing death. Many nights I have died on stage, but it is always preferable that a man die standing on his own two feet than it is for him to live life on his knees. And just like the Trap, the highs make it all worth it. The rush of a meticulously crafted joke killing before a packed house is akin to receiving a text from Sal, thousands of miles away in a Jersey stash house, letting me know the package has arrived safe. All the odds are against me, yet still I emerge victorious. I suppose comedy is the only thing keeping me out of the Trap — but for how long?

I'm sweating, my palms itch, and there's a gleam in my eye. Once a junkie, always a junkie. Only trouble now is, the weed racket is gone. After a century of prohibition, America has finally decided it wants to stop dancing. That's when Medellín called.

A year and a half after the riots at Umatilla, I returned home to find a message waiting for me. It was from Maria, who'd recently been released from federal custody in Cartagena. After Andres got clipped, the Colombian Federal Police seized our hotel in Taganga and Maria went on the lamb, hiding out with some guerillas in the remote jungles of southeastern Colombia. She eventually turned herself in — but not before making a pact with the guerillas, who'd recently renounced their revolutionary ambitions and turned their focus to cocaine production.

Unable to pin her for the murder of Andres Gaviria, Maria was charged with aiding and abetting a drug trafficking organization. After spending over a year in federal custody, on the eve of her extradition to the United States, the government abruptly dropped the charges, citing insufficient evidence. Whether it was a lack of evidence or the briefcase full of American cash Maria's attorney handed over to the head prosecutor as the two shared cigars at the exclusive Cartagena Yacht Club, one can only speculate.

Now, she's relocated back to Medellín, where each month she shuffles a metric ton of guerilla cocaine from the jungle to the coast, and then onward to New York City.

"I can get forty thousand a kilo in New York," she'd bragged to me over the phone.

Her English has improved remarkably in the years since our affair.

"*Pero*, I sell to you for twenty-five. You can be the exclusive gringo distributor of *La Nueva Medellín* cocaine in the United States."

It was a hell of an offer — selling $100 grams, just two of these kilos sucked up Wall Street banker noses every month could soon bring me enough to buy my own building on the Upper East Side.

"What happened to us?" I sighed. "I thought we were gonna leave this game behind so we could be together?"

She giggled, and for a moment I was reminded of the girl I once knew.

"*Aye, amor.* That would have been so nice. But dreams change, *ju* know that better than anyone. I hope tha'*ju* become a big star, but if *ju* ever change your mind, *ju* know where to find me."

Another gut shot, and the room pops with laughter. I just got the one-minute light and I'm gearing up for my big closer — the one about jail and getting a balloon of heroin stuck up my ass. Sure, I could close with one of my hits, something safe and relatable, but I'm a junkie alright — addicted to the thrill. I duck, jab with my left, then throw a hard right hook. It's a knockout punch. The laughter starts from the back of the room and then washes forward and onto the stage like high tide, soaking me in glory. Sorry, Maria. I'm infatuated by the Trap, but the love I have for this laughter is unconditional.

I suppose I'll live to see another day, and experience another moment. I guess I'll give life one last shot. Nothing better to do, anyway. In the end, we're all just inmates on planet Earth, spinning laps on the yard until the day our bus arrives to take us away.

This game is a motherfucker — I've told you the best way I know how. Do you finally understand?

No, I didn't think so. This is only for the hustlers.

The End

About the author

John Mitchell was born and raised in Portland, Oregon. In 2012, after spending two years in a maximum-security prison for drug trafficking, he moved to Los Angeles, where he is an active stand-up comedian and podcaster. "Days of the Trap" is his first book.

He hopes to stay out for good.

IG: @mrjohnnymitchell

Podcast: "Here's Johnny!"

CPSIA information can be obtained
at www.ICGtesting.com
Printed in the USA
LVHW021620170322
713568LV00012B/1273